The S
Pennines
40 favourite Walks

The authors and publisher have made every effort to ensure that the information in this publication is accurate, and accept no responsibility whatsoever for any loss, injury or inconvenience experienced by any person or persons whilst using this book.

published by
pocket mountains ltd
The Old Church, Annanside,
Moffat DG10 9HB

ISBN: 978-1-907025-73-0

Text and photography copyright © Alastair and Matthew Ross 2019

The right of Alastair and Matthew Ross to be identified as the Authors of this work has been asserted by them in accordance with the Copyright, Designs and Patents Act 1988

A catalogue record for this book is available from the British Library

Contains Ordnance Survey data © Crown copyright and database 2019 supported by out of copyright mapping 1945-1961

Printed in Poland

Introduction

Forming a great hill ridge down the middle of the North, the Pennines have earned the nickname 'the Backbone of England'. Rising in the north of Derbyshire, they run all the way to the Tyne Gap, just south of the border with Scotland. Along the way, their geology and natural history have produced some of our most iconic landscapes.

The area of the South Pennines detailed in this book fills the gap between the more frequently visited National Parks of the Peak District to the south and the Yorkshire Dales to the north. Wedged in between these popular parks, the region has often been overshadowed, but offers many rewards of its own. There is a rich tapestry of lush valleys, hills, moorlands and characterful settlements teeming with historical interest. In its own way, much of this landscape often rivals the serene wilderness of the National Parks.

A key feature of the South Pennines region is the boundary between Lancashire and Yorkshire, a watershed in both geographical and cultural terms! Rivers flowing west ultimately join the Mersey and the Ribble, while to the east the Aire, Colne and Calder are all tributaries of the Humber. The many streams and rivers rising on the hills have also been used to feed canals and reservoirs, meeting the needs of the nearby industrial cities. Manchester, Leeds and Bradford are all on the foothills of the region and so the South Pennines have

historically been criss-crossed by transPennine routes. Packhorse tracks, roads, canals and railways all tell tales of human endeavour through the ages, and mill towns like Huddersfield, Burnley, Hebden Bridge and Halifax sprang up along their routes. For the modern visitor, the proximity of these towns, cities and transport links serve to make the area easily accessible for exploration.

Natural history

The Pennines are characterised by coarse sandstone, often known as 'millstone grit'. These sedimentary rocks originated in river deltas that covered Britain roughly 320 million years ago. The deposits of mud and sand left by the rivers were, over time, compressed into hard layers of sandstone and shale. Later, tectonic movements pushed the rock upwards into hilly formations, and glaciers weathered them into their broad, smooth shapes. The deep valley trenches characteristic of the region were gouged out later by glacial run-off.

These valleys are now populated transport corridors, but their upper sides have remained too steep for extensive development. As a result, they retain peaceful ancient woodlands of oak, birch and holly. Within these are an array of small tumbling cloughs with tributaries which hold a wonderful air of lush, mossy enchantment.

By contrast, the gentler slopes above

are generally devoid of trees. Initially fields of rough grass used for grazing, they revert to tussocky moorland as the terrain becomes too wild for farming. It's hard to imagine now, but these areas were once very different, being covered in vast swathes of pine trees and juniper bushes. Over centuries, widespread deforestation by humans combined with heavy rainfall led soils to become waterlogged and acidic, decayed vegetation turning into peat. The result was the moorland now familiar to us, rough land of heather and rushes, punctuated with peat groughs.

There is a highly specialised flora and fauna adapted to living in these harsh conditions. The bobbing heads of cottongrass dominate wet places and, in less acidic areas, the whole of the hills turn purple in high summer thanks to the carpet of heather and bilberry. In summer, sheltered spots buzz with insects like the bilberry bumblebee and green hairstreak butterfly, and the sky is full of birdsong. This is a nationally important area for groundnesting birds, with many waders flying inland to breed in spring after a winter on the coast. The evocative call of the curlew and aerial acrobatics of lapwings are a joyous sign that spring has definitively arrived!

Smaller species include the skylark, meadow pipit and nationally rare twite. Raptors, such as the kestrel, merlin and short-eared owl, can also be found. Many of these species are at the extreme southern edge of their range, resulting in some parts of the moorland being designated Special Areas of Conservation. Despite this, it is perhaps surprising to learn that the South Pennines region as a whole is our only upland area to have no overall protection status. This may change soon, with proposals to create England's first 'Regional Park' in the area.

Moors and mills: the South Pennines through the ages

There is a rich history of human endeavour in the South Pennines. Despite the harsh conditions of the uplands, people have found ways to exploit the landscape for its natural resources, a tradition continuing to this day. Incidentally, although the history of the area is long, the name 'Pennines' is a surprisingly recent appellation, thought to date from 19th-century comparisons to Italy's Apennine range.

Traces of the earliest Neolithic settlement are found in standing stones and other antiquities. There is a particular concentration of these on Rombald's Moor, between the Aire and Wharfe Valleys. Later, the Romans built roads and forts to cross the hills in their efforts to quell the Britons. Other historic crossings are found in the causeway stones of ancient packhorse routes such as Rape's Highway or the several 'Long Causeways'.

Farming endeavours from early settlement resulted in deforestation of the moors, leaving the terrain we now know. However, the poor soil has always made arable farming challenging here, meaning efforts have focused on livestock. The Inclosure Act of 1773 intensified attempts to 'improve' and parcel up the land. The result was the now familiar mosaic of rough grass fields with drystone walls. The desperate attempts to claim every scrap of potential farming land in often unsuitable terrain can be seen in the evocative remains of abandoned farmsteads and tumbledown walls at the highest fringes of human habitation.

The lack of arable land led farmers to be creative, and a cottage industry of weaving sprang up in hilltop settlements. Weaving cottages survive throughout the area, recognisable by their rows of upper-storey windows, designed to allow extra light into weaving rooms. The ready supply of water helped develop the nascent industry through the construction of watermills, but this really kicked into high gear with the Industrial Revolution of the mid-19th century. At this time, huge mills were constructed in the valleys. Canals and railways brought much greater ease of trade and transport to the towns and linked up the hilltop farms with the woollen mills in surrounding cities. Housing also sprung up at this time to provide for the burgeoning populations of the developing mill towns, and these soot-blackened stone terraces have come to be a defining feature of the area. The hills above saw changes too, with widespread quarrying and reservoir construction to help feed the developments below.

After the slow and lingering death of the mill industry in the mid-20th century, the South Pennines have had to reinvent themselves. Gradually, the cloud of smog over the North of England has lifted and damage from industrial pollution has been repaired. Mill towns like Keighley, Halifax and Huddersfield are now seeing new life, while other settlements like Hebden Bridge and Haworth are popular tourist towns, and the surrounding countryside is attracting more and more visitors.

Progress continues to leave its scars – motorways, pylons and windfarms are all recent controversial examples. With such close proximity to centres of population, the South Pennines will always be a landscape under pressure, but the interaction between people and place here has left a fascinating mosaic of history.

Walking the South Pennines
On a clear day, with hills and moorland stretching in front of you for miles, or in pockets of deep green woodland, the South Pennines are quite breathtaking. There is great variety in the landscape, from the verdant valley floors to peaceful farms and rugged hills above. Plenty of natural and historical detail helps retain interest, and the elevated nature of the landscape provides many fine views.

All areas are well-served by paths, with farm tracks and quiet lanes also providing pleasing options. The reader will come across two notable long-distance routes several times in these walks: the Pennine Way and its Bridleway equivalent, which both follow the north-south ridge of the hills. There has been a lot of recent investment in these routes, so sections that were once quagmires or rutted tracks are now well-paved stone paths and tracks. There are many shorter-distance routes too, including the Mary Towneley Bridleway Loop or the Stanza Stones trail, which navigates between a series of slabs engraved with poems by Simon Armitage. Additionally, most councils have their own waymarked trails, such as the Calderdale Way, Pendle Way or Bradford Millennium Way. Of course, it is perfectly possible to navigate your own bespoke route using the network of paths, tracks and lanes. In addition, most of the upper reaches are designated Open Access land, which offers great freedom to explore. Do be aware on these sections of grouse shooting, livestock grazing and the potential for moorland fires; if you're a smoker, please carry a pouch for cigarette butts!

While the South Pennines aren't as mountainous as other northern regions, they are still upland areas and as such should not be underestimated. The wet climate produces above-average rainfall, and winters can be hard. The terrain may become waterlogged, and becks and rivers swell in response to weather. Mist and fog can occur all year round, providing an enigmatic air of majesty to the hills, but also the potential for confusion on the moors. As with all hillwalking, dress appropriately with waterproof clothing and stout footwear. A map and compass must also be carried, even if you use GPS. This is especially important on the higher-level routes, where paths are sometimes fainter. The maps in this volume are a good guide to the route, but should be used in conjunction with more detailed maps such as the OS Explorer series.

Public transport

Many walks can be accessed by public transport and using the bus or train also gives you the opportunity to undertake linear expeditions.

Trains

Two key transPennine rail routes pass through the South Pennines region. The Standedge route runs high frequency express trains between Manchester, Huddersfield and Leeds. Local trains on this route serve stations in the Saddleworth and Colne Valley regions, including Marsden and Greenfield, providing access to several of the walks in these areas.

The Calder Valley Line takes an alternative route between Leeds and Manchester, via Halifax and the towns of Calderdale. It splits between Hebden Bridge and Todmorden into two routes,

one heading over the Pennines to
East Lancashire, the other veering down
through Littleborough and Rochdale.
There are three trains an hour between
Leeds and Manchester, and one between
Leeds and Preston, as well as a direct
service from Burnley to Todmorden
and Manchester.

Frequent trains on the Airedale Line
connect Ilkley and Keighley with Leeds
and Bradford.

Buses

There is a wide selection of buses making
most lower-level areas accessible, and
climbing onto the higher fringes of the
hills, unreachable by rail.

Key routes for reaching some of the
locations by bus include:

- **180/1** Huddersfield – Marsden
  – Uppermill – Manchester
- **314** Huddersfield – Holmfirth – Holme
- **354** Ashton – Stalybridge – Saddleworth
  – Denshaw
- **356** Saddleworth Rambler (Greenfield –
  Uppermill – Delph – Dobcross)

- **589** Burnley – Todmorden
  Littleborough – Rochdale
- **590** Halifax – Hebden Bridge
  – Todmorden – Littleborough
  – Rochdale
- **592** Halifax – Hebden Bridge
  – Todmorden – Burnley
- **596** Hebden Bridge – Blackshaw Head
- **901** Hebden Bridge – Ripponden
  – Huddersfield
- **906** Hardcastle Crags – Hebden Bridge
  – Widdop (summer weekends and
  Bank Holidays)
- **B3** Keighley – Haworth – Oxenhope –
  Hebden Bridge (Brontë Bus)
- **M4** Burnley – Colne – Cowling
  – Keighley (Mainline)
- **X58** Halifax – Ripponden
  – Littleborough – Rochdale

Others are mentioned in each walk.

Information

There are tourist information and
visitor centres sprinkled throughout
the region, including in Hebden Bridge,
Todmorden, Holmfirth, Halifax, Ilkley
and Uppermill.

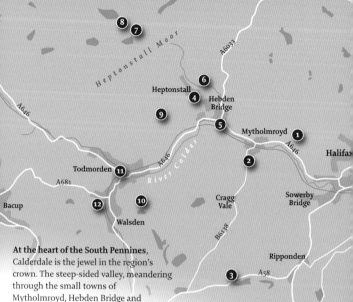

At the heart of the South Pennines, Calderdale is the jewel in the region's crown. The steep-sided valley, meandering through the small towns of Mytholmroyd, Hebden Bridge and Todmorden, is cloaked in lush, ancient woodland. Above the treeline, a flat contour opens up into fields, rougher pasture and heather moorland as you climb higher.

Rich in history, the Calder Valley was a cradle of the cloth industry. A bustling weaving business in hilltop villages like Heptonstall moved to the valley below when the Industrial Revolution took hold, the tumbling waters of the Calder and its tributaries ideal for powering mills.

A transport corridor also developed, with canal, road and rail all vying for space with the river. With limited space on the valley floor, settlements quickly had to spread up the steep valley sides. This left a characteristic array of tall, soot-blackened terraced houses clinging tenaciously to the hillsides, stacked like painted scenery for a play.

Their mills now silent, the towns of Hebden Bridge and Todmorden have reinvented themselves. With bustling arts movements at their heart, they revel in an individual way of doing things, manifested in vibrant communities and local businesses, and are very pleasant places to explore. For the walker, however, the real joy of Calderdale is found in the cascading cloughs feeding the river, enchanted mossy woodlands or the hillsides above offering panoramic views over the whole scene.

Calderdale

Luddenden Dean

Distance 7km **Time** 2 hours 30
Terrain a mixture of country lanes, tracks
and paths through woods and fields
Map OS Explorer OL21 **Access** bus (574)
from Halifax and Booth stops about 1km
from the start

The valley of Luddenden Dean is one
of the prettiest in Calderdale, as well as
being rich in history. This circular walk
explores both the main valley and some
of its hidden corners. Along the way you
pass historic mills, peaceful woodland
and the remnants of grand houses, with
an ascent to the hilltop village of
Wainstalls offering a panorama over the
whole scene.

Start at Jerusalem Farm car park,
reached from Luddenden Foot on the
A646 between Halifax and Hebden Bridge.
This is a council-owned nature reserve
and campsite with some of the oldest
natural woodland in Calderdale. From the
far end of the car park take the track
signed for the Wade Bridge and Calderdale
Way down to the bridge. On the far side
bear right to take the path slanting up the
bank. Keep straight ahead when the
Calderdale Way turns sharp left and keep
going through Wade Wood until you pass
a tranquil millpond on the left. Beyond
this ascend the steep steps, crossing a
track halfway up, until you reach a lane.

Turning left along the lane here, walk
uphill past a row of cottages at Jowler.
Just after the driveway to Hock Cliff, look
for a gap in the wall on the left and follow
the path around the side of the slope just
above the drive. Pass above and alongside
the house, going through two gates, and
then continue along the track to meet a
road. Turn left and then, just before the
bridge, notice steps on the right. A few
metres further along the road is the Cat
I'th Well pub. Its name apparently derives
from a corruption of 'Catherine's Well',

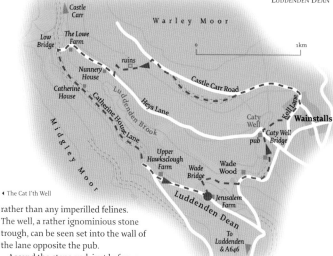

◄ The Cat I'th Well

rather than any imperilled felines. The well, a rather ignominious stone trough, can be seen set into the wall of the lane opposite the pub.

Ascend the steps and, just before a walled section of green lane, take another set of steps up to the right, then walk up through fields to Kell Lane. Turn left, ascending past the cottages of Tongue End to Wainstalls village. Turn left again at the top of Kell Lane, leaving Wainstalls and following the road around the side of the hill. This is the edge of the open moorland; in spring and summer curlews fly overhead and the banks of bilberry provide sustenance for pretty little green hairstreak butterflies.

Take the track on the left; this runs parallel to, and ultimately rejoins, the road. About 100m later a path enters the field on the left, passing the shell of a marooned railway wagon to follow a beck downhill. It curves through the stone ruins of New Hey Farm, before descending diagonally to a stone stile. The route now

runs along the edge of Upper Hey Wood. Just before crossing a small clough, turn left by a marker post and follow the route down through the trees. Exiting the wood at a lane, turn right to pass Nunnery House. The road then curves round to an imposing castellated gatehouse. This was once the entrance to the enormous Castle Carr mansion, demolished in the 1960s. Curve to the right along Catherine House Lane, passing under the gateway arch.

Follow this pleasant lane along the side of the valley. After about 1.5 km, it joins onto the elbow of a bend in another road. Turn left downhill past Upper Hawksclough Farm, where Bob's Tearoom is open at weekends. Shortly afterwards you will spot Jerusalem Farm car park on the left.

Land of the Coiners

Distance 8km Time 2 hours 30
Terrain firm tracks and field paths, a few
muddy sections Map OS Explorer OL21
Access Mytholmroyd is served by regular
trains and buses

The cloughs and woods of Cragg Vale are
tranquil today, but in the 18th century
the area was home to the Cragg Vale
Coiners, a notorious gang of forgers
who still loom large in local folklore.
This route weaves up and down the
valley, and through ancient woodland.

Leave Mytholmroyd along New Road
(B6138), following it for roughly 1km. This
road is the longest continual ascent in
Britain, rising around 300m in 8km and,
after being part of the Tour de France, it's
a popular route for cyclists. Immediately
before the road crosses Cragg Brook, take

the signed concrete 'Link Path' leading off
to the right. This climbs parallel to the
steep-sided ravine of Parrock Clough
before emerging into meadows. Ignore a
fork to the right and continue uphill.
A cattle grid heralds your arrival into
Broadhead Clough Nature Reserve.
Crossing a track, continue along the
footpath, signed for Erringden Moor,
straight ahead. The climb through this
lush woodland of twisted oak, birch and
alder is aided by stone steps in places.

Eventually, the path meanders to the
top of the treeline, emerging onto open
moorland, dotted with cottongrass and
yellow spikes of bog asphodel in summer.
At the fingerpost turn left for Bell House.
There are fine views back over the valley
as a series of marker posts take you
around the rim of Broadhead Clough.

These lead to a concrete track, passing
above Bell House, an isolated smallholding
which was once home to 'King' David
Hartley, head of the Cragg Vale Coiners.

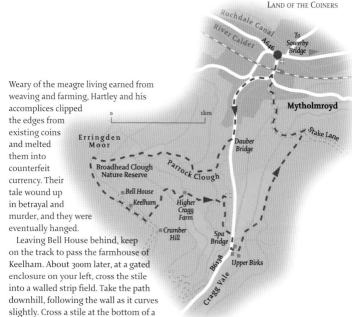

Weary of the meagre living earned from weaving and farming, Hartley and his accomplices clipped the edges from existing coins and melted them into counterfeit currency. Their tale wound up in betrayal and murder, and they were eventually hanged.

Leaving Bell House behind, keep on the track to pass the farmhouse of Keelham. About 300m later, at a gated enclosure on your left, cross the stile into a walled strip field. Take the path downhill, following the wall as it curves slightly. Cross a stile at the bottom of a field to join a barrow track, then turn right, continuing downhill. At the far end of Higher Cragg Farm, go through the gate to the right and follow this path. It runs parallel to the track, ultimately rejoining it to descend steeply toward Cragg Brook.

Immediately before the brook, turn right along a riverside path. Pass a series of tumbling riffles to arrive at Spa Bridge, curtained with ivy. The eponymous spa was frequented by local millworkers but is now long gone. Turn left on the lane to cross the bridge and climb uphill to meet the main road. Go right, heading along the pavement for about 100m. Cross the road to enter the pocket-sized Cragg Vale

Park through a gate, signed for Holderness Wood. Exit the park by a gate and turn left up a lane between the cottages of Mid Birks and Twist Clough. Immediately behind Upper Birks cottages, turn left over a small lawn to join a walled footpath aiming for the woodland.

A gap in the wall ahead leads into the wood. Keep climbing until you reach the top of the woods. From here, the path follows the rim of the valley with fine views. Ignore all turns and eventually a gap in the wall by a sign gives access to Stake Lane. Turn left to descend this cobbled track, which morphs into Hall Bank Lane and continues downhill to Mytholmroyd.

◀ Above Broadhead Clough

Great Manshead

Distance 9km Time 2 hours
Terrain moorland paths Map OS Explorer
OL21 Access bus (901) from Huddersfield
and Hebden Bridge runs past the start

Great Manshead Hill forms a great wedge
of high ground between the Ryburn
Valley and Cragg Vale. Wide skies and
distant panoramas generate a sense of
freedom as you stride over this lofty
moorland, but despite its wildness there
are plenty of reminders of human
interaction with the landscape.

The A58 crosses the Pennines between
Halifax and Rochdale, reaching the top at
Blackstone Edge. There is a lay-by about
3km east of this summit, just above the
end of Baitings Reservoir. From here,
cross the road to find a stile leading to a
permissive path, signed for Manshead Hill
and Waterstalls Road. This path crosses

and then climbs along the side of
Greenwood Clough, soon passing the
house at Manshead. Continue up the
clough, re-crossing its small beck twice.
Towards the head of the valley, and
entering open moorland, veer right and
keep ascending, with occasional posts
marking the path clearly evident on the
ground. A final steeper section gains the
edge of the plateau next to a stone cairn,
from where it is a short hop to the trig
point on Manshead End (447m).

Enjoy the extensive views from here,
mist permitting! You will spot various
human monoliths piercing the horizon:
Stoodley Pike to the northwest; Emley
Moor TV mast to the southeast; even the
cooling towers of Ferrybridge power
station 50km to the east. But these are
dwarfed by the big skies and the overall
vastness of the moors.

Keep on the path past the trig point, crossing the wide featureless ridge of Great Manshead, but basking in the views. The valley to the right leads down to Cragg Vale. It is claimed that this stretch of road is the longest continuous ascent in England, rising steadily for about 8km between Mytholmroyd and Blackstone Edge and gaining about 300m in height. Descending from Great Manshead the path eventually comes alongside a wall and levels out to reach a junction of tracks next to a ruined brick construction. This was a Second World War bunker which was part of a decoy system designed to draw bombers away from nearby industrial targets. It is difficult to conceive how Nazi bombers would have mistaken boggy Pennine moorland for the railway marshalling yards at nearby Greetland! But the Starfish decoy system included a range of pyroclastic activities designed to confuse and mislead. The hummocks and hollows hereabouts are remnants of past quarrying, giving the area its name of Slate Delfs Hill.

At the junction, turn right and take a good track gently downhill. Just past a small plantation, pass through a gate and meet a lane. Turn right and walk along this quiet and pleasant road, as it rounds the head of Blackshaw Clough. After about 1km, and just after a right-hand bend, go over a stile next to a gate, and take the track, signed as a Yorkshire Water permissive path. Pass a small plantation, then veer left as the track becomes a path. This keeps gradually rising across the flank of Great Manshead for over 1km, intermittently soggy underfoot, but with no serious issues. It reaches the plateau at Manshead End, with the trig point just off to the right. The stone cairn on the edge of the ridge is the marker for the descent along the outward route.

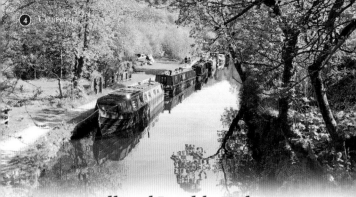

Heptonstall and Jumble Hole

**Distance 8.5km Time 3 hours 30
Terrain a mixture of country lanes, tracks
and paths through woods and fields
Map OS Explorer OL21 Access regular bus
(596) from Hebden Bridge to Heptonstall**

**The steep valley sides around Hebden
Bridge are cloaked with lush woodland,
hiding a series of delightful cloughs and
tumbling streams. This walk takes in
valleys, hillsides and historic settlements.**

Start at the public car park at Heptonstall
Social & Bowling Club. Turning left out of
the car park, take a path curving downhill
with views along the valley as you emerge
onto the shoulder of the hill. The rocky
path leads down to a junction, where a
sharp left continues the descent through
oak woodland. Cross Heptonstall Road and
follow it downhill to the right for roughly
200m. Just after a bus stop, go down the
Cuckoo Steps via a gap in the wall on the
left to the main road below. Crossing the
road, turn left and then immediately right,
in front of the Co-op supermarket.

Cross the canal bridge at Hebble End,
turning right up New Road at a T-junction.
Climb stiffly over Weasel Hall railway
tunnel and towards Horsehold. Just as the
road emerges from the woods and starts to
level off, take a signed public footpath to
the right, by a telegraph pole. This opens
up to Horsehold Scout, a rocky outcrop
with views across the mills of Hebden.

The path now follows the edge of the
steep valley side, before descending
gently through beechwoods to the
cascading stream of Beaumont Clough.
Rough stepping stones help you ford the
beck; after crossing, take the path through
Callis Wood. As a house appears, bear
slightly left to join the Pennine Bridleway.
Continue downhill towards the Rochdale
Canal. Cross Callis Bridge, continue over
the River Calder and cross the main road.

To the left, the bridleway continues as a
track set back from the busy road. Turn
right at Jumble Hole Road, following it
under the railway bridge and straight on
to Jumble Hole Mills. A concrete track

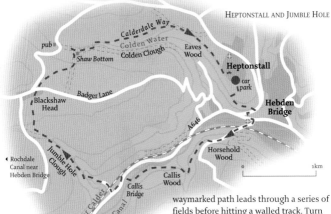

leads you up into this charming wooded clough, where a series of watermills now quietly recede into mossy greenery. At a junction, turn left to cross a bridge over the stream, then follow the track as it doubles back and climbs steeply. At the next bend where the track veers left, continue your trajectory by taking the path clinging to the steep side of the beck.

After an ascent through woods carpeted with bilberry and sedge, you arrive at a T-junction with another path. Bear right to the evocative ruins of Staup's Mill. Just beyond is a footbridge; cross it and climb out of the woods.

When you reach a wall and signpost, turn left in front of the wall, pass through a gate and turn right along the Calderdale Way. This farm track leads to the settlement of Blackshaw Head. On meeting the road here, cross it and take a gated path slightly to the right. This well-waymarked path leads through a series of fields before hitting a walled track. Turn left, heading downhill towards Colden.

Just past Shaw Bottom House, turn right at the T-junction and continue for about 350m. At a marker post on the left, take a path leading down to a small bridge over the beck. The path divides shortly after crossing it; take the left fork up stone steps. A short distance later, ignore a second set of steps to the left. Instead, follow the Calderdale Way along the edge of the bank, leaving the woodland by a stone stile and crossing fields until you reach a tarmac lane.

Turn right here and almost immediately follow the path around the back of some houses. Stick to the well-marked Calderdale Way posts, bearing slightly left and down to a walled path, then joining a lane uphill. A subsequent path on the right leads through Eave Woods. Initially narrow and rocky, it soon opens up to a grassy edge with fantastic views of the valley. Turn left in front of a wall at the entrance to Hell Hole Rocks and follow the path back to Heptonstall.

Hebden Bridge and Stoodley Pike

Distance 12km Time 3 hours 30
Terrain tracks, quiet lanes and paths of
variable quality; some may be muddy
Map OS Explorer OL21 Access Hebden
Bridge is well served by trains and buses

**A walk exploring the distinct layers of
the Upper Calder Valley, starting in the
valley floor settlement of Hebden Bridge.
Ascend the steep wooded valley sides to
gain access to the contour shelf above,
dotted with historic farms and wonderful
viewpoints. The high, rough moorland is
home to the totemic, obelisk-shaped
Stoodley Pike Monument, a silent sentry
overlooking the valley below.**

From the centre of Hebden Bridge,
follow signs to the railway station, a
restored Victorian gem. Keep to the left-
hand side of the main booking office
entrance, dropping down to join a lane
passing under the railway bridge. Follow
the lane to the right, Wood Top Road, as it
ascends the hill through mossy woodland
and then weaves through the buildings of
Wood Top Farm. Then continue upwards
along the cobbled track, Spencer Lane.

As the hillside levels out, follow the
main track through the historic buildings
of Old Chamber, avoiding any turn-offs.
The swift climb from Hebden Bridge now
rewards you with excellent views across
the Calder Valley to Heptonstall. Other
rewards may be found at a small 'honesty
box' café, offering self-service hot drinks.

Leaving Old Chamber behind, follow
the rough cobbled track as it turns to
the left, beneath some powerlines.
Continue on this track, straight across a
tarmac road; Stoodley Pike now appears
on the horizon. The route remains fairly
flat as it passes along the shelf of the
Calder Valley, once the valley floor before
glacial meltwater carved the deeper
trench of the current valley. The shelf has
the best pasture land and hosts a
number of historic farms, including
Erringden Grange.

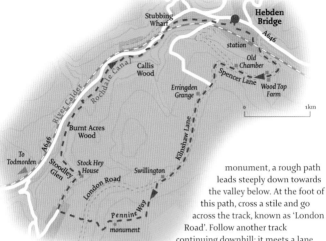

Shortly after the last farm at Swillington, the track comes to a junction. Take the Pennine Way on the left, up the hill towards Stoodley Pike. The path ascends from rough pasture to moorland; curlews, reed buntings and skylarks may be seen here. Pass through a drystone wall, take a right turn and continue to Stoodley Pike Monument, now looming above you. The 37m-high monument is actually the second on this site. The original, erected in 1815 to celebrate the defeat of Napoleon, was destroyed in a storm in 1854; its 1856 replacement additionally commemorates the end of the Crimean War. It may be ascended by an internal staircase to a balcony offering fine views.

From the entrance side of the monument, a rough path leads steeply down towards the valley below. At the foot of this path, cross a stile and go across the track, known as 'London Road'. Follow another track continuing downhill; it meets a lane next to the former Stoodley Hospital. Turn right along this lane and continue as it narrows, ignoring turnings to the side. The lane ends at Stock Hey House, where a short path leads to a beck in the small valley of Stoodley Glen.

Ford the beck and continue on the public bridleway, signposted Burnley Road. The concrete track follows the tumbling glen through woods of birch, beech and oak, turning into a lane next to the Rochdale Canal. Just before the lane crosses the canal, take a footpath off to the right, signposted Burnt Acres Wood. Shortly afterwards this path forks; take the lower option. When the path meets the canal, loop under the bridge and join the towpath, continuing for around 3km, past Stubbing Wharf and back to Hebden Bridge.

Hardcastle Crags

**Distance 7.5km Time 2 hours 30
Terrain tracks and good paths
throughout with gradual ascents and
descents Map OS Explorer OL21
Access summer weekend bus (906) from
Hebden Bridge**

The National Trust estate at Hardcastle
Crags spreads across the twin valleys of
Hebden Water and Crimsworth Dean. In
Edwardian times it was called 'Little
Switzerland' and was prized as an escape
for workers and their families from the
smoke and grime of the mills in Hebden
Bridge and Halifax. Deep wooded
cloughs, cascading becks and mature
woodland combine to offer a magical
terrain with many paths and waymarked
trails offering a range of alternative
walking expeditions to suit all abilities.

The two valleys which make up the
Hardcastle Crags National Trust Estate are
a haven for wildlife. Mixed woodland,
millponds, streams and meadows
combine to provide habitats for dippers,
herons and roe deer, to mention but a few
species. Start from the National Trust car
park at Hardcastle Crags. This is the main
car park at the entrance to the woods at
Midgehole, reached by leaving the A6033
on the way out of Hebden Bridge. There is
a charge for non-members. Take the track
signed to Gibson Mill, passing the
information point in a wooden shelter.
The main track crosses the mixed
woodland above the valley bottom and
arrives at Gibson Mill in 2km. An
alternative waymarked route, the Mill
Walk, reaches Gibson Mill using a
narrower path close to the riverbank.
Snuggled in a clearing at the water's edge,
it was built in 1800 and was one of the
earliest cotton mills. A century later, it
became a focus for day visits and

◄ Gibson Mill

entertainment. Today it still welcomes visitors and is totally self-sufficient in energy and water. Displays inside recall some of its former life as an industrial and recreational venue. There is also a café and National Trust shop.

Beyond Gibson Mill, the track begins to rise, passing among rocky outcrops. These bluffs are the original 'Hardcastle Crags', though the name is now applied to the whole valley. A signed footpath on the left opposite a clearing allows you to explore the crags. Ignore a left fork taking waymarked routes down to the river and keep ascending on the main track until you emerge above the trees at a junction. To shorten the walk, you can turn sharp right here and follow the track as it contours around the edge, then drop down the hillside into Crimsworth Dean. For the main walk bear left to join the track, following it around a left-hand bend, over a beck and on to the hamlet at Walshaw. Just before the collection of houses, turn sharp right through a

gate to take a bridleway, signed for Crimsworth Dean.

Enjoy the distant views as the track rises across the flank of the hillside. Later it crosses to the other side of the moor wall and soon afterwards begins to descend. The track becomes a walled lane as it leaves access land and drops to a T-junction next to a ruined farmhouse perched high above the valley of Crimsworth Dean.

Turn right here, the track running across the hillside and then gradually descending through dappled woodland to reach the car park and the start.

21

Walshaw Moor and Blake Dean

Distance 9.5km **Time** 3 hours
Terrain a combination of hard tracks and
some narrower moorland paths
Map OS Explorer OL21 **Access** summer
weekend bus (906) from Hebden Bridge

Some of the most remote and
captivating country in the South
Pennines surrounds the upper reaches
of Hebden Water. No fewer than six
reservoirs capture the generous
precipitation over these moors, which
are bisected by an old packhorse route,
now a moorland road, between Hebden
Bridge and Colne. This circular route
explores the high grouse moors and
deep wooded cloughs so characteristic
of these haunting uplands.

Start from Clough Foot car park on the
road between Hebden Bridge and Colne.
Take the signed Pennine Way footpath up
from the car park to join the Walshaw

Dean Reservoirs access road. This rises for
a short distance and then continues into
the valley of Walshaw Dean, with its three
reservoirs built to slake the thirst of
Halifax. Continue for 1km, then turn right
to leave the access road on the signed
Pennine Way and cross the dam of the
Lower Reservoir.

On the far side, turn left on a narrower
path until it passes the end of the Middle
Reservoir dam. Beyond this pick up a
broad track veering away from the water
and rising onto the grouse moor. At a
T-junction, turn right, winding up to the
top of the hill. Enjoy a panoramic view
across the high Pennines, with the
evocative cry of the curlew and the croak
of the grouse resonating across the
heather. Keep on the track as it weaves
downhill, ignoring side turnings, with the
deep wooded defile of Hardcastle
Crags in the distance ahead.

Walshaw Dean
Middle Reservoir

Walshaw Dean
Lower Reservoir

Wadsworth Moor

Clough
Foot

Pennine Way

To
Colne

car park

White Hill

Alcomden

Gorple
Lower
Reservoir

Pack
Horse Inn

Graining Water

Blake
Dean

To
Hebden Bridge

Overwood

Walshaw

Hebden Water

0   1km

Reaching the small settlement of Walshaw, keep straight ahead to find a stile and footpath next to the entrance to a barn on the left. Cross the yard and descend a field next to a fenced wall to find a small gate in the bottom corner. A lovely path now descends steeply through the woodland, above a cascading beck on the left. At the bottom, turn right onto a track into the upper reaches of Hardcastle Crags, just above the Hebden Water. When the track ends at a house, Overwood, keep ahead on a path beyond. This meanders through woodland, then negotiates a short rocky section where you may need an occasional steadying hand. A little further on, notice the footings of a bridge in the beck below. The construction of the Walshaw Dean Reservoirs involved building a 9km narrow-gauge railway from Heptonstall, which leapt across the valley here on a trestle bridge. The path makes use of the old track bed for a little while before

heading diagonally down to the confluence of becks at Blake Dean. Cross the footbridge and enjoy the setting of this popular local picnic spot. Shortly beyond this climb a few steps to the road at Blake Dean Bridge.

Turn right onto the road and climb the hill for about 200m to the first hairpin bend. Leave the road here and keep straight ahead to cross a stile at a public footpath sign. An interesting path rises diagonally through bracken and beneath crags to reach the rim of the valley. Pass above the confluence of the Reeps Water and the Graining Water, veering right but keeping close to a wall. In a little while, the flagged footpath of the Pennine Way sidles in from the valley to the left. Soon afterwards, about 100m short of a house, the path turns right to cross the field to the road. Turn left to follow the road back to Clough Foot.

Widdop and Gorple

Distance 6.5km Time 2 hours
Terrain good tracks with a stretch of
moorland path and quiet road
Map OS Explorer OL21 Access summer
weekend bus (906) from Hebden Bridge
to Widdop

The northwestern area of Calderdale
holds some of its wildest moorland
regions. Much of the area has special
protection and is home to a range of
birdlife, including the relatively
uncommon twite.

Six reservoirs have been used to
capture the abundant water from the
upper reaches of the Hebden Water.
They were built between the 1870s and
1930s to meet the demand from the

developing industrial towns. This walk
visits three of these reservoirs. Although
it's relatively short and easy, it's also a
real taster of the wild secrets of the
South Pennines.

The road between Hebden Bridge and
Colne is an old packhorse route and
crosses some of the remotest country in
Calderdale. Widdop Reservoir sits
alongside the road, about halfway
between the two towns, and was
constructed for the Halifax Corporation
between 1871 and 1876. There is a car park
on the roadside about 150m from the
dam. From here a footpath runs parallel
to the road to reach the reservoir.

Turn left and cross the dam. Once
across, the track at first hugs the

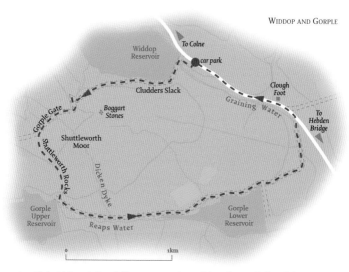

To Colne

car park

Widdop
Reservoir

Cludders Slack

Clough
Foot

Graining Water

To
Hebden
Bridge

Gorple Gate

Boggart
Stones

Shuttleworth
Moor

Shuttleworth Rocks

Dicken Dyke

Gorple
Upper
Reservoir

Reaps Water

Gorple
Lower
Reservoir

0   1km

waterside but later winds uphill, away from the reservoir, onto the moors that divide Lancashire from Yorkshire. The dark weathered rocks of Cludders Slack brood over the landscape but also provide a challenge for rockclimbers. Heather, bilberry and bracken shroud the massive boulders cluttering the steep hillside. This is the route of the modern Pennine Bridleway but it has far greater antiquity in the form of Gorple Gate, an ancient transPennine crossing. A stiff climb brings the stony track onto the high moorland, accompanied by the sound of red grouse, curlew and skylark. Extensive views open ahead into Lancashire, as well as southwards across Calderdale to Stoodley Pike.

A signpost is reached near the track's highest point. Turn left, along the signed permissive path for Upper Gorple.

A rough but clear path threads its way down through Shuttleworth Rocks, aiming for the dam of Gorple Upper Reservoir in the hollow below.

On reaching the dam wall, turn left to follow the track, signed for Lower Gorple. The pleasant reservoir access road runs down alongside Reaps Water to reach Gorple Lower Reservoir, passing a few small plantations with rowan and silver birch trees.

Lower Gorple was built from 1927 and a narrow-gauge railway linked the two reservoirs during the construction period. At Lower Gorple dam, turn left, rejoining the Pennine Bridleway. Follow the track to the road at Clough Foot, perhaps with nesting peewits wheeling overhead to dissuade intruders. At the road, turn left, passing Clough Foot Farm and continuing to Widdop.

◄ Widdop Reservoir

Colden, Rodmer Clough and Noah Dale

**Distance 7.5km Time 2 hours
Terrain mostly firm tracks and field
paths, a few muddy sections Map OS
Explorer OL21 Access regular bus (596)
from Hebden Bridge**

Calderdale was scoured out by glacial
floodwater thousands of years ago,
carving a steep-sided trench from the
Pennine watershed towards the North
Sea. Above this, the original valley floor
has been left as a 'shelf' just below the
highest moorland, often hosting the
oldest settlements in Calderdale. Colden
is such a hanging valley; it borders a
remote upland above the treeline but has
been settled for centuries by scattered
dwellings and farms. This walk explores
a mesmerising landscape, using ancient
tracks and field paths.

Start at Jack Bridge, next to the New
Delight pub near Blackshawhead. This is
reached from the unclassified Hebden
Bridge to Burnley road, known as the
Long Causeway. Between the pub and the
bridge, a narrow lane labelled 'Jack Bridge'

leads off the road, between the beck and a
row of cottages. A gentle ascent takes the
lane above the valley floor, weaving
among scattered farms and converted
barns. Just above Nettlebed Farm, at a
junction of tracks, turn right onto the
Pennine Bridleway for Gorple Reservoir.
Enjoy views back down the Colden Valley
towards Heptonstall Church, before the
path drops through mature woodland,
passing Land Farm on the right. The
remarkable landscaped gardens have been
created 300m above sea level in a harsh
Pennine environment. At least 20,000
trees have been planted and over 50
species of bird recorded. The grounds are
open to the public on some weekends
between May and September for a modest
entry fee. At the end of the gardens, just
before the beck crossing, turn left onto
the signed public bridleway.

An excellent track follows the water and
then rises steadily into Rodmer Clough,
winding up the wooded recess past a
small pottery and some adjacent houses.
Double back to cross the beck and ascend

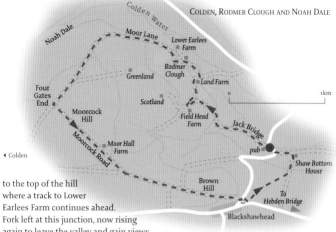

to the top of the hill where a track to Lower Earlees Farm continues ahead. Fork left at this junction, now rising again to leave the valley and gain views across the wide moorland all around. This is rough country, just a short distance from the Pennine watershed, but it's crisscrossed by a network of tracks and bridleways that ease progress. The farms carry evocative names, such as Scotland, Greenland and Egypt, and the shallow valley to the right is Noah Dale. A steep ascent brings the track to a gate at Three Gates End. On a clear day Pendle Hill and Ingleborough are visible on the northern horizon through gaps in the nearer hills. Carry on for a further 300m to the next junction and then turn left (no sign) at Four Gates End.

A rutted, walled track soon conquers the modest dome of Moorcock Hill, the highest point of the walk at 431m. From here it's a steady and gradual descent with panoramic views across Calderdale. The obelisk on the horizon is Stoodley Pike, built to celebrate peace after the Napoleonic Wars. Further on in distance

and time, the TV mast at Emley Moor is visible to the southeast. Maintain this general direction for about 2km, ignoring turnings, on a combination of hard-core track and grassy bridleway. Pass the houses of Blackshawhead a short distance to the right before arriving at the road near a chapel.

Turn left and walk along the road for a short distance, then turn right just before the bus stop. A narrow tarmac lane runs alongside the graveyard for 100m before reaching another road. Turn left and almost immediately go through a field gate on the left. The path, part of the Calderdale Way, traverses a sequence of fields and descends into the valley. At a crossing with a walled track, turn left to follow this steeply downhill, past Shaw Bottom House, and on to a T-junction. Turn left here and follow the track up to the road, turning right to arrive back at the New Delight.

Gaddings Dam and Langfield Edge

Distance 7.5km **Time** 3 hours
Terrain mostly well-defined paths over
hillsides and moorland
Map OS Explorer OL21 **Access** bus (T6, T8)
from Todmorden to Lumbutts

**In a commanding position above
the Upper Calder Valley, the remote
Gaddings Dam was built to collect water
for the Rochdale Canal and local mills.
These days its outflow is sealed and the
water is purely aesthetic, but the
reservoir enjoys local celebrity thanks to
its small sandy beach. Beyond Gaddings,
the walk along Langfield Edge gives a
skylark's-eye view of the area's industrial
legacy and the valley beyond.**

Start at the Methodist chapel in
Lumbutts. There are roadside parking
places here. Better still, get the bus from
Todmorden. As the road bends right,

downhill to the village, a track leaves it
straight ahead. Follow this track around a
tree-lined millpond, one of a sequence left
as reminders of the village's industrial
past. As the track curves through Lee
Farm and its outbuildings, another relic
appears: the semi-derelict waterwheel
tower of Lumbutts Mill. Built in 1830, the
30m-high tower housed three large
waterwheels powering the mill. When the
track rejoins Lumbutts Road, turn left and
follow the lane uphill for roughly 500m.

Just before the Shepherd's Rest Inn,
take the Pennine Bridleway on the left.
Ignoring a subsequent turning to the left,
keep on the stone-flagged path, known as
Salter Rake. It snakes its way onto the
nape of the hill, with Walsden and the
Upper Calder Valley now in sight below.
At a marker post, turn left along a rough,
grassy path ascending the hill. The path

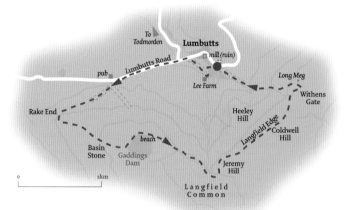

passes the Basin Stone, a prominent rock formation whose name is derived from weathered holes in its flat surface. This enigmatic feature was once used as a pulpit by travelling evangelists, including John Wesley. Continue ascending gradually towards Gaddings Dam, now appearing ahead. This is actually Gaddings West, one of two reservoirs built here in the 1830s. Joining the dam wall, follow it to the left until you reach the 'beach' in the opposite corner. This small sandy corner of the reservoir results from erosion of the underlying gritstone. It's not quite Camber Sands, but the novelty value was sufficient to turn the remote spot into a millworkers' playground. It still remains a popular local spot to this day, so much so that a local group bought the reservoir in 2001 to prevent it being drained. Gaddings East Reservoir had already suffered this fate; arriving at the beach, you will see its

empty shell in front of you. Take the path along the wall of the abandoned dam, continuing along this as it drops past the old outflow, then passes above a quarry. Stone for the dams was quarried from here, allegedly by convict labour.

Follow the path around a nick containing a small stream, then continue along Langfield Edge towards Stoodley Pike. The path ascends slightly to Coldwell Hill, a tussocky area patrolled by meadow pipits. Clusters of large rocks herald the approach of the Pennine Way; join it and keep working your way towards Stoodley Pike as the path dips a little, then rises again.

At a crossing of paths near a lonely boundary stone, turn left downhill. This is a good quality path of causeway stones weaving downhill, with Lumbutts now back in view. At a junction with another track, continue your descent, arriving back onto the lane at the chapel.

◀ Gaddings Dam

29

Rocks and cloughs of Todmorden

Distance 10km **Time** 3 hours
Terrain moorland and woodland tracks,
steep in places **Map** OS Explorer OL21
Access buses and trains from Halifax,
Burnley and Rochdale to Todmorden

Todmorden is a border town with an
independent spirit and ambiguous
identity. Sitting where three valleys meet,
it is an ideal base for exploring the upper
reaches of Calderdale with its sequence of
wooded ravines, or cloughs. On the high
moors, fantastic rock formations have
been weathered from millstone grit.
This walk is a great introduction to a
fascinating and complex landscape.

From the centre of Todmorden, walk up
Burnley Road for about 400m. Opposite
the entrance to a primary school, turn
right into Victoria Road. Just after the
railway arch, take the second left up
Meadow Bottom Road. At the end of the
houses, fork left to keep ascending past
the Coach House. Bend right at a junction
to stay on the bridleway as it curves uphill
past a disused quarry to reach a junction
of paths next to a small bridge.

Curve round to the left here, joining the
Calderdale Way, now rising less steeply
towards East Whirlaw Farm and Cally Hall
Farm. As the track turns sharp right into
Cally Hall Farm, turn left and follow a
path contouring round the hillside for the
next 1km. Pass just above East Whirlaw
Farm and notice the boulders and crags of
Whirlaw Stones to the right.

After about 1km, and about 200m short
of a ruined shelter, bear left by a marker
post to take another walled track
diagonally downhill towards some farm
buildings. Pass the farm and notice the
startling rock formations of Orchan Rocks
on the hillside ahead. Where the farm
road turns sharply left to avoid a wooded
ravine, leave it and bear right to find a
little path over the head of the ravine,
Stannally Clough. Go through a small iron
gate, cross a strip of woodland, then walk
alongside a field to reach the farm at
Lower Hartley.

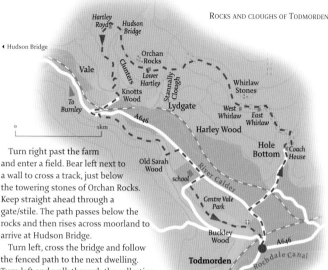

◄ Hudson Bridge

Turn right past the farm and enter a field. Bear left next to a wall to cross a track, just below the towering stones of Orchan Rocks. Keep straight ahead through a gate/stile. The path passes below the rocks and then rises across moorland to arrive at Hudson Bridge.

Turn left, cross the bridge and follow the fenced path to the next dwelling. Turn left and walk through the collection of attractive buildings at Hartley Royd. Through the gate, a track leads downhill, passing a mast and then curving around the edge of a precipitous drop into the tangled wooded valley of Clunters. The path weaves down into Knotts Wood, eventually coming to a sharp bend and junction by a post. Turn sharp left here, almost doubling back, continuing downhill. Reaching Knotts Road, turn sharp right and follow this down to the main road.

Turn left along the main road for about 100m, then almost opposite a small water pumping station, turn right, cross the River Calder and immediately bend left along a lane. As it approaches a house, go through a gate to the right, taking a path rising across the hillside. After the next stile, take the left or lower option at a

fork, which later rises to cross a track coming downhill. Turn left here and follow the track, descending into Old Sarah Wood.

At the bottom, turn left, then pass the caravan dealer to reach the main road and turn right. Just after Todmorden High School, turn right to leave the main road on the signed cycleway and footpath to Todmorden town centre. Pass the swimming pool, turn left and continue to follow the cycleway along the bottom of Ewood Wood and Buckley Wood into Todmorden, passing above Centre Vale Park and enjoying good views across to Stoodley Pike. As you come into the town, descend the Ridge Steps, going under the railway and into the town centre.

Gorpley Clough and Inchfield Moor

Distance 11km **Time** 3 hours
Terrain paths of varying grade, from
gravel towpaths to one rough section
over moorland **Map** OS Explorer OL21
Access regular buses (589, 590) from
Rochdale and Todmorden to the start

Once part of Lancashire, the area around
Walsden now forms the furthest reaches
of West Yorkshire. The tumbling becks
that originate on Inchfield Moor twist
through the delightful cloughs at
Ramsden and Gorpley to reach the valley
below, ultimately draining into the River
Calder in Todmorden.

Start in Gauxholme, 1km south of
Todmorden, by the junction of the A6033
and A681. A few metres up Bacup Road,
turn right into Peckswood Road, then
almost immediately take a footpath
doubling back on the left, signed as the
Todmorden Centenary Way. The spiralling
ascent of this grassy path offers
impressive views down to the Gauxholme
railway viaduct below. Further afield is

Todmorden, its incongruously classical
town hall watching over the rest of the
town. Reach a tarmac track swinging away
from the valley, passing a mast. About
100m later, look on the left for a stile next
to a metal gate, waymarked Todmorden
Centenary Way Link. Follow a series of
yellow waymarks to descend the field.
At the bottom, turn right through a gate.
Reaching a fork, take the lower path on
the left. Immediately afterwards, arrive
at a crossing of paths next to a farm
building; here take the right-hand path
going across the fields. Exit the pasture
through a metal kissing gate to enter
Stones Wood. Cross a tumbling clough
before descending gently to meet with
Bacup Road.

Turn right along the road for about
100m to a small car park at the foot of
Gorpley Clough. Take the path on the
left-hand side of the car park, signed for
Gorpley Wood. It nestles next to the
stream, criss-crossing it on a series of
bridges. This clough is one of Calderdale's

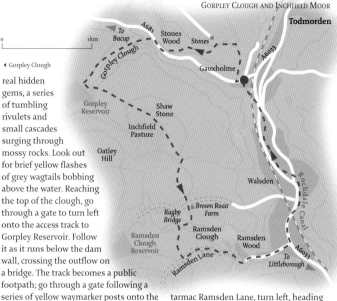

◀ Gorpley Clough

real hidden gems, a series of tumbling rivulets and small cascades surging through mossy rocks. Look out for brief yellow flashes of grey wagtails bobbing above the water. Reaching the top of the clough, go through a gate to turn left onto the access track to Gorpley Reservoir. Follow it as it runs below the dam wall, crossing the outflow on a bridge. The track becomes a public footpath; go through a gate following a series of yellow waymarker posts onto the rough hillside pasture.

A faint path climbs gently towards the top of a broad moorland swelling; a compass may be needed in mist. Aim slightly to the right of stones visible on the crest of the ridge (known as the Shaw Stone). As the farmhouse at Brown Road Farm becomes visible straight ahead, use this as a guide across the pasture. Shortly before the farmhouse, join a track from the left, pass a small pond and continue straight ahead between the farm buildings. Walk down the grassy track through trees into Ramsden Clough. Cross the stream here by means of Ragby Bridge, then ascend the footpath to the other side of the clough. On meeting the tarmac Ramsden Lane, turn left, heading downhill to ultimately meet Ramsden Wood Road going on to meet the main road in Walsden.

Turn left. It's a short walk past the garden centre and mill shop empire of Gordon Rigg. As you pass a garage on the right side of the road, look for an unmarked path leading between the left side of the garage and a house. This short cut-through leads to the Rochdale Canal at Nip Square Lock. Turn left along the towpath for a pleasant 2km canalside walk, punctuated by a road crossing at Bridge 32. Continue to Gauxholme Highest Lock. Immediately after this is Bridge 31; exit here to your start point on Bacup Road.

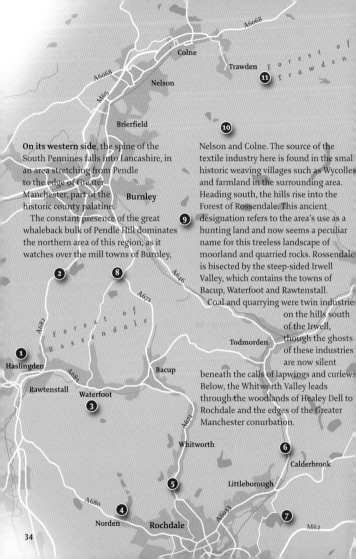

On its western side, the spine of the South Pennines falls into Lancashire, in an area stretching from Pendle to the edge of Greater Manchester, part of the historic county palatine.

The constant presence of the great whaleback bulk of Pendle Hill dominates the northern area of this region, as it watches over the mill towns of Burnley, Nelson and Colne. The source of the textile industry here is found in the small historic weaving villages such as Wycoller and farmland in the surrounding area. Heading south, the hills rise into the Forest of Rossendale. This ancient designation refers to the area's use as a hunting land and now seems a peculiar name for this treeless landscape of moorland and quarried rocks. Rossendale is bisected by the steep-sided Irwell Valley, which contains the towns of Bacup, Waterfoot and Rawtenstall.

Coal and quarrying were twin industries on the hills south of the Irwell, though the ghosts of these industries are now silent beneath the calls of lapwings and curlews. Below, the Whitworth Valley leads through the woodlands of Healey Dell to Rochdale and the edges of the Greater Manchester conurbation.

Lancashire's South Pennines

Haslingden's Halo and Cribden's crown

Distance 8.5km Time 2 hours 30
Terrain firm tracks and paths around the
hill with narrow moorland paths along
the crest; some sections may be squelchy
Map OS Explorer OL21 Access frequent
bus (464) from Rochdale and Accrington

Cribden Hill rises steeply above
Rossendale and its broad crown offers
spectacular views across Lancashire. On
the western edge of the hill, a steel 'halo'
overlooks the valley, one of a series of
sculptures symbolising the regeneration
of East Lancashire. A circular walk links
these two highlights, starting from an
attractive Victorian park.

The main entrance to Whitaker Park is
on Haslingden Road (A681), less than 1km
west of Rawtenstall town centre. There is
parking available inside the park and
along the roadside. Walk up through the
park, weaving along the pathways to the
top entrance opposite the entrance to the
ski slope. Turn left along Haslingden Old

Road for about 150m to reach the exit from
the ski centre. Look out for a footpath sign
just beyond and take the path uphill at the
side of the ski centre until you come to a
T-junction with a track.

Turn left, rising gradually around the
hillside, wide views stretching
southwards across the Irwell Valley with
the A56 snaking towards distant
Manchester. You may even spot a wisp of
smoke from the steam engines on the
East Lancashire Railway. The track
gradually curves around the slope of the
hill, turning northwards. At a fork next to
a house, bear right, keeping uphill on a
rutted footpath. Cross a small road at Top
o'Slate and just beyond this a gate leads
left off the path to reach the Halo.
Rossendale's answer to the Angel of the
North, the Halo is one of a series of
panopticons built across East Lancashire.
The high steel lattice, 18m in diameter,
rises above the hillside.

Return to the track and continue north

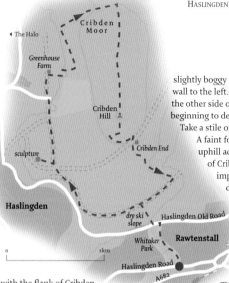

Cribden Moor

◀ The Halo

Greenhouse Farm

Cribden Hill

sculpture

Cribden End

Haslingden

dry ski slope

Haslingden Old Road

Whitaker Park

Rawtenstall

Haslingden Road

A682

0   1km

slightly boggy crest of the ridge, with a wall to the left. The right of way swaps to the other side of the wall and then, after beginning to descend, approaches a fence. Take a stile on the right here.

A faint footpath heads gradually uphill across the rough tussocks of Cribden Moor but soon improves and offers 360-degree views across a broad swathe of Lancashire as it strides across the crown of the hill. The summit is passed without drama and shortly afterwards the path goes through a metal gate. Turn right immediately after this and head steeply downhill next to a wall. At the bottom, next to a metal gate, turn left along the track which contours around the base of the hill.

At a fingerpost, turn sharp right, doubling back along a bridleway which slants down the hillside and through a small copse. Pass between a barn and farmhouse. The bridleway continues next to the right-hand wall of the house and drifts steadily downhill through a series of fields with a grand panorama of Rawtenstall ahead. On reaching a stony track, turn right and follow this until you reach the top of the ski centre, turning left to return by the outward route to Whitaker Park.

with the flank of Cribden Hill rising to the right. After a short descent, accompany a small stream and then cross another small road. Keep ahead along Laund Lane for about 100m and then turn right onto the signed public footpath in front of Green House Farm. Cross several stiles and on the rough grassland above the farm follow several waymark posts leading left to a track. Follow the track past a ruined barn and through a gate. Turn left here, taking the right of way just above a wall along the hillside, soon passing a few farms and houses. By the last of these houses, a footpath sign points ahead over a stile. Ignore this, instead veering uphill to the right just before the stile. At the top continue across a stile and traverse the

Dunnockshaw and Clowbridge

Distance 10km Time 3 hours
Terrain lanes and mostly good tracks,
much across moorland Map OS Explorer
OL21 Access regular bus service (X43)
along the A682 from Manchester,
Burnley and Nelson

A wide moorland pass links the deep
cleft of Rossendale to the wider skies of
Pendle and the Ribble Valley. In past
centuries, packhorses carried lime and
other goods along this important trading
route and the hamlet of Gambleside
occupied the land around the highest
point. The settlement declined after the
completion of Clowbridge Reservoir in
1866. This tour takes in the high ground
on either side of the valley, including the
weather station on Hameldon Hill and
the Dunnockshaw Community Woodland
with many excellent paths and tracks to
explore freely. Many trees have been
planted here, although the walk is
mainly across open moorland.

Clowbridge Reservoir is the base for a
sailing club and the car park is a good
starting point for the walk and close to
the nearest bus stop. Be aware that it
closes in the evening. From the car park
entrance, cross the main road and walk
right (north) along the pavement for
about 250m. At the end of the row of
houses, turn left, signed for the Weather
Station. This narrow and barely used road
rises diagonally across the rough hillside,
heading for the masts and 'golf ball' that
comprise the weather station at the top of
the hill. On the final section of the ascent,
the road bears left, but an alternative
stone track keeps straight ahead, rising
parallel to the road, and soon reaches the
weather station crowning the summit of
Hameldon Hill.

Where the road ends by one of the
masts, keep straight ahead on a track.
The trig point lies a short way to the right
and is out of sight of the track. But the
route ahead lies along a broad ridge,

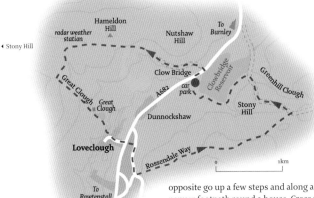

with excellent views across Rossendale to the south and over the Forest of Bowland and Pendle to the north. Go through a gate, keeping on the main track as it curves downwards and left to a further gate. A walled track leads beyond, descending gradually to arrive at a marshy, level area after about 350m. Watch out for a ragged junction at this point, with two rights of way leaving the track to go left. Take the first of these which descends rough pasture with a fence just to the right. A path soon becomes more evident as it drops towards the house at Great Clough. Continue beyond the house onto the tarmac driveway leading down to the village of Loveclough. At the beginning of the village, turn left at a T-junction and then bend round to the right, staying on the lane until it meets the main road.

Cross the road and almost exactly opposite go up a few steps and along a narrow footpath round a house. Cross the small field to reach a lane beyond. Turn right along the lane for about 400m. Just after the junction with Green Fold Drive, leave the lane, turning left along a signed public bridleway. There is a gradual rise along the path, now the Rossendale Way, initially alongside a small wooded valley and then across unimproved pasture and grassy moorland. It is easy going with extensive views in all directions.

About 2.5km after leaving the road, arrive at a track crossing, just underneath a line of pylons and next to a stone cross. Turn left and follow the stony track across the level ground of Stony Hill and then downhill towards the reservoir. Immediately in front of the water, turn left onto a concessionary path alongside the reservoir. (Be aware that dogs are barred from this footpath, but an alternative is to continue to the main road and follow this on the far side of the reservoir.) This deviates round the sailing club and returns to the car park.

Valley of Stone

Distance 7km Time 2 hours 30
Terrain stone tracks with one steady
ascent and descent Map OS Explorer OL21
Access frequent buses (464) from
Rochdale and Accrington to Waterfoot

Quarrying in Rossendale stretches back
centuries, but it was during the 19th
century that the industry mushroomed.
Demand for the hard sandstone that
makes up the bedrock of the land led to
the creation of vast sprawling quarries
across the hillsides, served by a network
of tramways. A horseshoe route above
the side valley of Cowpe gives insights
into the remains of Cragg Quarry, as well
as offering wide views across Rossendale
to Pendle Hill and beyond.

Waterfoot sits astride the main valley
road between Rawtenstall and Bacup.
Cowpe Road leaves the main road at a

mini roundabout, just a few metres east
of the traffic lights in the centre of the
village. There is a small car park on the
right just after the beginning of the road.
From here walk along Cowpe Road past
the health centre, then bear left up Carr
Lane, passing Waterfoot pumping station.
Keep straight ahead as the road becomes
Hartland Drive until you come to the end
of the road. Just past the last house, go
through a gate onto the bridleway
beyond. Follow this all the way along the
field edge, curving round to the left, until
you reach a gate in the top left corner.
A stone track lies on the other side. Turn
right along this, rising towards the mast
ahead. Pass through a farmyard before
arriving at a road junction next to a
second mast.

Turn right, taking the broad stone track
known as Rooley Moor Road. This was an

◄ Cowpe Reservoir

important medieval wool-trading route between Rochdale and Whalley Abbey, but sections were also laid during the 19th-century cotton famine. After about 600m, just next to a deep quarry hole with a pond in the bottom, bear right through a gate to take another stone track which rises gradually across the head of the Cowpe Valley, with the reservoir in view far below. At the top, go through a gate to join the Pennine Bridleway at the entrance to Cragg Quarry. Turn right and soon bear left to follow the main bridleway through the middle of the disused workings. The quarry once covered a vast area of the hilltop and is now enjoyed by mountain bikers as part of the Lee Quarry trail centre. The mountain biking routes are on distinct tracks, mostly separate from the main bridleway. At first the route traces a groove through the stone but later it contours the edge with extensive views north. An information panel explains the gauge tramway system that facilitated the excavations between 1867 and 1920, taking rock to the valley floor via an incline.

At a junction, fork right, staying on the Pennine Bridleway and soon reaching a marshy col in front of the grassy dome of Cowpe Lowe ahead. Bear right here on the Pennine Bridleway, signed for Waterfoot. The track now weaves down the hillside, with trees replacing moorland as height is lost. It emerges onto the road through Cowpe. Turn left and walk along this the short distance to Waterfoot, though take care as there is no footway in places.

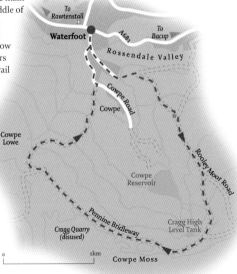

41

The Naden Valley

**Distance 6.5km Time 2 hours 30
Terrain firm tracks and good paths
almost all the way round
Map OS Explorer OL21 Access frequent
bus (442) from Rochdale to the main
road, 500m from the start**

The Naden Valley forms a deep cleft in
the high moorland plateau between
Rochdale and Rossendale. Once a milling
and farming community, it was flooded
to provide a series of four reservoirs for
nearby Rochdale. Today footpaths
encircle the dale, offering tranquillity
and solitude with opportunities to see a
range of birdlife on the water, including
goosander and even egrets.

Leave the A680 Blackburn to Rochdale
road at the White Lion pub in Norden,
turning north along Over Town Lane.
After about 400m look out for the metal
gates at the entrance to Greenbooth
Reservoir. You can park on the lane close
to this point. Walk through the pedestrian

gate and follow the tarmac driveway over
the dam. Greenbooth was the last of the
reservoirs to be built in the valley and
only dates from the 1960s. The village of
Greenbooth, now beneath the water,
suffered after the closure of the mill in
1911 and some people moved, seeking
work elsewhere. In the end, 80 homes and
a school had to be flooded to make way
for the reservoir, whose dam is more
than 35m high.

At the far side, turn left through the
metal gate and follow the surfaced path as
it rises steadily above the reservoir. Views
open out across the water to the quarries
on the far side and the mighty wind
turbines of Knowl Moor perched on the
horizon. Silver birch and pine trees clothe
the slopes down to the water's edge.

Arriving at a junction with a track, bear
left downhill on this reservoir access
drive, which descends diagonally above
the imposing pile of the former
waterboard house. The promenade offers

◀ The Naden Valley

a fine panorama of the upper valley. At the bottom the track curves across the dam of Naden Middle Reservoir. Immediately before crossing the dam, turn right through a gate to take a path alongside the water. The three Naden reservoirs were constructed in the 1840s, over a century before Greenbooth. Although it's no distance from Rochdale, there is a real sense of remoteness, tucked away in a hidden trench in the hills, with shades of green and brown from the grass and bracken. At the end of the Middle Reservoir, marker posts guide the way up the edge of the steep and grassy dam of the Higher Reservoir. Bear right and continue along the path around its perimeter to the head of the dale. A footbridge carries the path over the inflow, a convergence of the Naden Brook and Ding Clough.

The return route now lies along the opposite side of the water, becoming a surfaced track. Where this turns to cross the dam of the Middle Reservoir, leave it and keep straight ahead through a gate, taking the footpath beyond. It straddles a shelf above the reservoir and beneath the imposing rocky face of Dixon's Brow. Further on, above Greenbooth Reservoir, the path bears right, climbing steeply to gain a higher-level footpath, running above the rocky quarried sides of the reservoir. Stay on the path, dropping down some steps to cross a small wooded

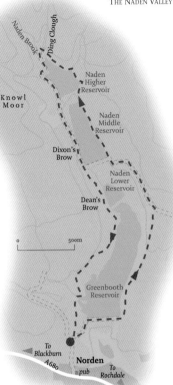

clough. Beyond this stay on the main footpath next to the fence. A further switchback takes you in and out of a deep defile, next to an impressive waterfall. Steps lead up the edge of a housing estate and a path will take you behind the houses and back to the road where the walk started.

Healey Dell and Cowm Reservoir

Distance 10.5km Time 3 hours
Terrain mainly good tracks but
including sections of exposed moorland
Map OS Explorer OL21 Access regular
bus (464) from Rochdale and Accrington
runs along the main road between
Whitworth and Healey Corner

The cotton mills that spawned the
industrial development of East
Lancashire have long gone. Dour but
captivating hills now cradle the River
Spodden as it winds through the
magical hidden woodlands of Healey
Dell. Industrial history surrounds every
step of this walk, from the remains of
a Victorian railway to the hollow of
Cowm Reservoir, etched into the mighty
Pennine Hills. There is an austere dignity
in this rugged landscape that richly
rewards exploration.

Reach the Healey Dell car park by
turning west off the A671 along Station
Road, just north of Healey Corner
between Rochdale and Bacup. You can
also start from Whitworth. Turn left out
of the car park and walk uphill on the
cobbled byway, passing a pond and soon
reaching the hamlet of Broadley Fold.
Keep straight ahead on the Pennine
Bridleway and then about 100m after a
large brick ruin take a track to the left,
leaving the bridleway. Bend left on
approaching a housing estate, then turn
right just before a reservoir wall. The path
contours above the housing before
descending to a T-junction at Fold Head.
Bear left here, ascending past Fold Head
High Barn and going through a gate onto
a track beyond.

A sunken path reaches the brow of a hill
to reveal a panorama of Cowm Reservoir,
tucked into a fold of the hills and backed
by the vast excavations of Britannia

◀ Cowm Reservoir

Quarry. Descend towards the head of the reservoir, where a picnic area offers a convenient respite. Join a track alongside the far side of the reservoir, noting the commemoration of James Treacle Sanderson, a local runner who died in 1905. Pass the dam and keep ahead along Tong Lane to reach the centre of Whitworth.

Turn left along the main road and almost immediately turn right into Acre Street. When the road veers left, keep straight ahead uphill on a track. At the sign for Mid Long Acres Farm, bear right, continuing uphill, alongside a wood and onto the moor. In a few metres, meet a hard-core track and turn right, contouring the hillside above Whitworth Church and below the golf clubhouse. In another 1km drop slightly into Clay Clough, arriving at a crossing of tracks in front of a reservoir retaining wall.

Turn right here, following the Rochdale Way to Healey Corner. Take great care crossing the main road here to the junction with Shaw Clough Road. Instead of walking up this road, bear right down a narrower side road descending into Healey Dell. The lofty stone arches of Healey Viaduct soon appear on the left, with eight arches leaping 31m above the wooded depths of the Spodden Valley. Immediately before the viaduct, take the footpath left, climbing steps to the

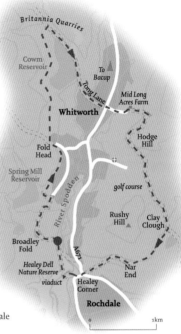

trackbed on the top of the remarkable structure. Turn right, crossing the viaduct and continuing along the former branch of the Lancashire and Yorkshire Railway opened in 1870. Pass the site of Broadley Station and, soon after passing under a roadbridge, watch out for steps to the left, leading back up to the car park and the start.

Crook Hill and Reddyshore Scout Gate

Distance 13km Time 4 hours
Terrain rough tracks and grassy paths
across open hills, exposed in places
Map OS Explorer OL21 Access buses (589,
590) from Todmorden and Rochdale

The wild hills above Littleborough are
blessed with bracing summits and terrific
views to the valleys below, as well as
revealing layers of human history from
antiquated packhorse routes and ruined
farms to Victorian reservoirs and more
modern exploitation of the landscape.

Start from the Summit Inn on the main
road between Rochdale and Todmorden.
Turning right (north) from the pub, cross
at the toucan crossing and immediately
turn left up the signed Pennine Bridleway
footpath. Meeting a tarmac lane at the
top, turn left to stay on the Pennine
Bridleway, which remains your guide for
the next 4km. About 200m later take the
right-hand fork uphill. Soon after,
continue along the sandy path leaving the
lane and then weave through a cluster of

farms. Shortly before a church, turn right,
signed for Shore. Climb slightly through
heather and bracken, continuing past the
farm at Grimes and meandering through
dips and cloughs. Pass the charismatic,
cartoon-shaped Ratcliffe Hill on your left.

About 150m later, just after a marshy
area and immediately before passing
under powerlines, turn slightly uphill
(right) at a fork to leave the Pennine
Bridleway. The rutted track rises onto
rough pasture and up to the nape of the
hill. Pass Turn Slack Dam on your right.
A small walled shelter heralds your arrival
on the crest of Crook Hill, but the summit
has much of its thunder stolen by the
gathering of wind turbines here. These are
just the latest in thousands of years of
human exploitation that has shaped the
upland landscape in places like this; the
hum and swish of their constant turn add
something of an otherworldly feel to the
hillside, especially on a misty day.

The route veers slightly left to pass
around the windfarms. Continue down into

From Reddyshore Scout Gate

a dip with a crossing of tracks at a boundary stone. Turn right here, along the Long Causeway. This antiquated packhorse route, once the main route between Rochdale and Todmorden, is now a quiet path across the moors. Continue on the causeway as it crosses the windfarm access track and passes through a wall marking the boundary between Greater Manchester and West Yorkshire.The Long Causeway continues, now slightly downhill, to meet another wall with an interpretation board on blanket bogs, and views down to Cranberry Dam. Following the line of the wall, you descend gradually and go through a metal gate onto a tarmac lane. Turn sharp right to double back and, just before the stone farmhouse of Ramsden Farm, turn right through a gate onto the waymarked Todmorden Centenary Way. As your route sweeps back below the hillside, look out for twite, the rare 'Pennine finch', and buzzards soaring above.

At the ruins of South Ramsden Farm, turn left. You pass near the reservoir at Cranberry Dam, crossing a stile to enter the end of White Slack Farm. Just after crossing a small beck, the path broadens into a track, with a delightfully incongruous little garden on your left

equipped with picnic tables for walkers where you can admire the deep gorge of Ramsden Clough below.

Carry on along the track as it drops down to a metal gate and joins a tarmac lane at Lower Allescholes Farm. Turn right along the lane. Just before Moorhey Farm, ignore the tarmac track; instead carry on along the rougher track around the rim of the valley. This is Reddyshore Scout Gate, another historic traders' route. At an old milestone, the Pennine Bridleway joins from the left. You now have commanding views of the Summit Gorge, with the Rochdale Canal below and Blackstone Edge on the horizon opposite. Joining a tarmac lane, bear right and immediately left to return to the Summit Inn.

Hollingworth Lake

Distance 6.5km Time 2 hours
Terrain excellent lakeside and field paths
Map OS Explorer OL21 Access train and
bus services from Calderdale, Burnley
and Manchester to Littleborough

Although built to provide water for the Rochdale Canal, Hollingworth Lake became a popular destination for 19th-century millworkers from neighbouring towns. It earned the nickname 'Weighvers' Seaport' and it's still a popular location today, with a range of attractions around the water and neighbouring countryside. This easy circular walk combines a circuit of the lake with an exploration of the wooded Ealees Valley.

There is plenty of parking in Littleborough and the walk starts from the far side of the railway station. From the town use the station subway to reach the road on the other side. There is a small lay-by parking area next to the Rochdale Canal. From here follow the canal towpath to the right, towards Rochdale. Opened in 1804, this was the first transPennine waterway linking Sowerby Bridge and Manchester, a distance of more than 50km. Like most of the inland waterways, the route faced decline and was closed shortly before the Second World War. A lengthy and vigorous campaign culminated in its reopening in 2002. It now forms part of the 111km South Pennine Ring, crossing the Pennines between Manchester and Huddersfield.

Reach the first bridge, Number 52, after about 700m. Leave the towpath here,

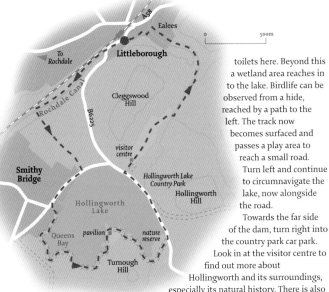

toilets here. Beyond this a wetland area reaches in to the lake. Birdlife can be observed from a hide, reached by a path to the left. The track now becomes surfaced and passes a play area to reach a small road. Turn left and continue to circumnavigate the lake, now alongside the road.

Towards the far side of the dam, turn right into the country park car park. Look in at the visitor centre to find out more about Hollingworth and its surroundings, especially its natural history. There is also another café here! Walk all the way through the car park onto a track beyond. As this bends right towards a small pond, follow the path that goes straight ahead across a wildflower meadow and picnic site. Beyond the pond, cross a footbridge and remain on the path along the Ealees Valley. Pass to the left of the stables, keeping on the track through woodland to reach the hamlet of Ealees. After you cross a road, a narrow path passes between hedges just in front of a terrace and soon reaches Lock 48 on the Rochdale Canal. Turn left, crossing the footbridge at the end of the lock. Turn left to follow the towpath back to the start.

turning left across the bridge and walking along a walled footpath beside a field. Over the brow of the hill, pass through a farmyard and onto the track beyond. This ends at a road in front of Hollingworth Lake, originally built as a watersource for the Rochdale Canal.

Turn right and follow the lakeside, passing the car park, cafés and watersports centre. At the far end of the Beach pub, take the track to the left, leaving the road and entering Hollingworth Lake Country Park. Continue alongside the lake edge on an excellent gravel path, crossing a dam and reaching the Pavilion with a café and

Thieveley Pike

Distance 9.5km Time 3 hours (shorter option also available) Terrain moorland paths and tracks with one steep climb Map OS Explorer OL21 Access no public transport to the start

Locals know well the wild attractions of the moors and the wooded cloughs in this less visited part of the South Pennines. Thieveley Pike crowns the moorland ridge, and the valley below is a key route through the area.

Start from the car park at Crown Point, about 5km south of Burnley, on a minor road from the A646. Crown Point lies on the ancient Salt Way running along the Pennines between Rochdale and Clitheroe. Its royal nomenclature probably relates to the recruitment of soldiers from nearby towns in the 18th century. Follow the surfaced footpath (signposted for the Panopticon) to the *Singing Ringing Tree*, one of a series of sculptures built across East Lancashire between 2003 and 2007. The wind resonates through the steel structure to compose a haunting musical drone. To its right, cross a stile (yellow waymark). A faint path veers left downhill, next to a wall on the right. There is a short squelchy section, but with careful footwork it is not as bad as it looks! A waymark indicates the route across a broken-down wall. Descend the next field with the remains of the wall on the left to reach the gate next to a house. Cross the stile and continue down the steep concrete driveway to the main road.

Almost opposite, just a few metres to the right, walk down a short flight of steps into the field. The path follows the right-hand side of a small beck to arrive at a stile next to Dyneley Cottage. Turn right along the broad track until it ends at some houses and a gate. Keep ahead here, through the gate and onto the Pennine Bridleway towards Holme Chapel, with blue waymarks for company. Pass another farm and ignore a left turn past a mobile phone mast. Stay on the bridleway until it burrows under the railway line through a small arch. On the far side, turn

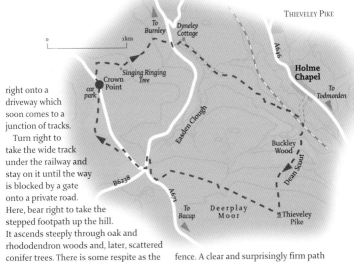

right onto a driveway which soon comes to a junction of tracks.

Turn right to take the wide track under the railway and stay on it until the way is blocked by a gate onto a private road. Here, bear right to take the stepped footpath up the hill. It ascends steeply through oak and rhododendron woods and, later, scattered conifer trees. There is some respite as the trees clear and the gradient eases. This is the site of Thieveley Farm, one-time venue for Bank Holiday trips, which was demolished in the 1930s. Sporting competitions, refreshments and fairground attractions drew weavers from local mills up the hillside from the railway halt at Holme Chapel. Keep ahead, ignoring side paths, and go through the kissing gate to keep ascending the rocky spur of Dean Scout. When the fence turns to the left, carry straight on along the faint footpath, soon crossing a broad track. Maintain this direction until the trig point appears. Thieveley Pike was once a link in a chain of beacons which were used to communicate important news over the Pennines.

Cross the stile a few metres to the left of the summit and then turn right to follow the path on the far side of the

fence. A clear and surprisingly firm path follows the ridge gradually downhill across Deerplay Moor for about 1.5km. It arrives at a gate in front of a main road. Immediately in front of it, turn right to join the Pennine Bridleway for 400m, roughly parallel to the road until it comes to a path junction by a cattle grid.

Go across the grid and through the gate onto the main road. Turn left and walk along the pavement for about 100m to a road junction. Turn right (signed for Rawtenstall) and immediately right again onto a minor road. Ascend this side road for about 350m to the brow of the hill. Here, turn left onto a track to shortly reach a gate. Just in front of it, turn right across a stile into Dunnockshaw Community Woodland, replanted as part of the Forest of Burnley project. Follow the path until it reaches the car park at Crown Point.

Shedden Clough and Hurstwood

Distance 9.5km **Time** 2 hours 30
Terrain moorland paths and tracks
Map OS Explorer OL21 **Access** nearest bus
(592) from Burnley and Todmorden stops
at Hurstwood

The moors above Burnley harbour both
inspiring scenery and an intriguing
history. This walk visits Shedden Clough,
once a hive of limestone extraction, and
the Tudor settlement of Hurstwood. The
moors give rise to the River Brun, after
which Burnley is named. Some
historians claim this remote upland was
the site of the decisive clash between the
Danes, Gaels and Anglo-Saxons at the
Battle of Brunanburh in 937.

Start at Maiden Cross car park on the
unclassified road between Burnley and
Heptonstall, about 3km east of
Mereclough. Nothing now remains of
the Maiden Cross itself, originally an
ancient route marker but named in
the 16th century after a woman
who came to the cross to mourn
the death of her lover in the English Civil
War. The horizon northwards
encompasses a sweeping view, from
nearby Pendle Hill to the more distant
profiles of the Forest of Bowland and the
Three Peaks of Yorkshire.

From the car park, go through the iron
gate and follow the track across the moor.
The path descends and comes to a
junction with the Pennine Bridleway. Bear
right here to join the long-distance trail
and continue down into Shedden Clough
where pockmarks and hummocks betray
an industrial past. Limestone was found
here, an erratic geological remnant left by
glacial action and quite uncommon in
this part of the Pennines.

The walled track weaves a route down
through the clough, turning right at the
bottom to cross a small footbridge.
Follow the right-hand side of a beck and
soon re-cross it by the stepping stones.
At the junction beyond, turn right onto
the Pennine Bridleway for Hurstwood
Reservoir, now crossing a stone bridge

and continuing along the track to reach the corner of Cant Clough Reservoir. Cross the dam wall and at the far side go through the iron gate. Keep ahead on the track, still the Pennine Bridleway, as it rises over hummocks and moorland and then drops towards Hurstwood Reservoir.

In front of the water, the track bears right along the water's edge. At the far end of the reservoir, turn left through a gate over a little footbridge (signed Burnley Way). The path rises a little above the reservoir and traverses a wood to reach a broad grassy terrace. On reaching the outflow, bear right to follow the path as it slants uphill. Look for a stile to the right on the opposite side of the narrow sliver of woodland. Cross this and turn left to follow an enclosed track as it twists quite steeply downhill to a kissing gate. Walk into the hamlet of Hurstwood, ensconced in the valley of the River Brun and once the home of Elizabethan poet, Edmund Spenser.

Historic Hurstwood Hall lies across the junction in the centre of the settlement. Just beyond the Hall, take a bridleway to the left. This drops into a small dell and crosses Foxstones Bridge. A good track gradually rises from the wooded valley to reach moorland, with views opening out. About 200m after the last house, Middle Pasture Farm, the track bears to the right. Leave it here and go straight ahead across a stile next to a locked gate (Burnley Way). After a short descent go through another gate and pass along the bottom of a small valley. Soon go through a kissing gate to join the Pennine Bridleway. Retrace the outward route, not forgetting to leave the Pennine Bridleway and bear left near the top of the hill to reach the car park.

Boulsworth Hill

Distance 9km Time 2 hours 30
Terrain exposed high-level moorland
with a mixture of good tracks and grassy
paths which are muddy in a few places
Map OS Explorer OL21 Access no public
transport to the start

Boulsworth Hill looms above East
Lancashire, its formidable profile capped
by a crown of jagged crags. An extensive
and confusing moorland wilderness
surrounds the summit, which is also
known as Lad Law. The massive bulk of
Boulsworth blocked the path of
glaciation in the last ice age, and
meltwater broke through to create the
nearby Cliviger Gorge. Until 2000 it was
impossible to visit Boulsworth legally,
apart from one permissive loop path
from the north. Today, this walk uses
open access land to traverse the moor
and explore the fascinating summit.

The moorland road between Hebden
Bridge and Colne dives down into the
head of the Thursden Valley about 7km
south of Colne. There is a road junction
next to a cattle grid at the bottom of the
dip and there are a few roadside parking
places near here. Take the Pennine
Bridleway south from here, signed 'MT
Loop, Gorple Road', for an immediate
steep ascent up the side of Rieve Edge.
'MT' refers to Lady Mary Towneley, who
initiated the creation of a 64km circular
trail based on old packhorse trails. This
particular section of the Pennine
Bridleway was opened in 2009. After about
1km, leave the bridleway as it turns right
at a fingerpost, instead going left, signed
for Rapes Clough. A level and squelchy
moorland path crosses the bleak terrain,
shortly reaching the Colne to Hebden
Bridge road at its summit.

Cross the road and keep straight ahead

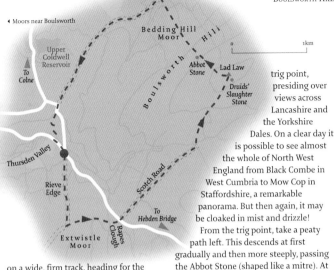

◀ Moors near Boulsworth

trig point, presiding over views across Lancashire and the Yorkshire Dales. On a clear day it is possible to see almost the whole of North West England from Black Combe in West Cumbria to Mow Cop in Staffordshire, a remarkable panorama. But then again, it may be cloaked in mist and drizzle!

From the trig point, take a peaty path left. This descends at first gradually and then more steeply, passing the Abbot Stone (shaped like a mitre). At the bottom, after crossing a marshy section, come to a broad track running along the base of the hill.

Turn left and walk along this bridleway which soon regains some height across the moor. After just over 1km, with Coldwell Reservoirs in view ahead, turn left at a junction to stay on the Pennine Bridleway, signed for Gorple Road. This arrives at the road above the Thursden Valley. Continue ahead along the road for a short distance, but where it bends to the left and starts to descend keep ahead onto the Pennine Bridleway through a gate, signed Gorple Road. It wiggles down the hill through a beechwood before emerging onto the valley road at the bottom. Turn left to reach the road junction and starting point.

on a wide, firm track, heading for the broad profile of Boulsworth in the distance. The track was engineered in the 1930s for the unlikely purpose of prospecting for oil. It is known as the Oil Track and also as the Scotch Road, and now serves as an excellent thoroughfare across the boggy surroundings. In 2km the track ends at the old oil well site. Look for a small footpath leaving the left-hand edge of this hard-core turning area. It crosses a small stream and heads across the moor, rising directly towards the jagged rocks on the summit of Boulsworth. After a final steep section, go across the first stile onto the summit area. Just to the right of the stile is the Druids' Slaughter Stone, alleged by some to have been a venue for ritual sacrifice. The summit itself is marked by a white

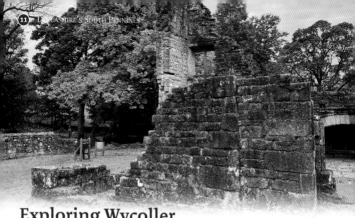

Exploring Wycoller

Distance 6km **Time** 1 hour 30
Terrain quiet lanes, farm tracks and
grassy footpaths **Map** OS Explorer OL21
Access no public transport to the start

An amble around the idyll of Wycoller.
This virtually car-free village is both
picturesque and rich in history. The
unusual bridges and buildings clustered
around the tumble of Wycoller Beck tell
a tale of human engineering through the
centuries. One of the true delights of
Lancashire, the village is surrounded by
equally lovely valleys and woodlands,
explored on this walk.

Start from Wycoller Country Park car
park (the lower car park, reached by a
signposted side road from Trawden).
A path reaches the village from here,
running parallel to the lane. Wycoller is
a charming gaggle of old stone cottages
wreathed in roses and honeysuckle.
The whole valley was bought by Colne
Corporation in 1896 with a view to

flooding the valley for a reservoir.
As a result, the village gradually became
deserted and derelict until 1972 when
ownership was transferred and the area
became a country park. The Aisled Barn
and ruins of the former Hall now add to
its charm and interest. There is also an
excellent café and visitor shop here.

The walk continues up the side of
Wycoller Beck. There are three choices of
crossing here: a ford and two bridges! The
slabs of the clapper bridge date from the
18th century, while the delightfully
lopsided arches of the Packhorse Bridge
go right back to the 15th century. Having
chosen your method of crossing, follow
the main track past the eerie ruins of
Wycoller Old Hall. This was reportedly
Charlotte Brontë's inspiration for
Ferndean Manor in *Jane Eyre*. Upon the
death of the last owner in 1818, the house
fell into ruin and was looted for its
stones. The ruins are open to wander
through, and enough still remains to

◀ Wycoller

enable you to conjure the past while walking through fractured arches and doorways. Like all good ruins, Wycoller Hall comes with reports of a resident ghost, the former owner, Squire Cunliffe! Returning to the present, continue following the track along the beck and pass the oldest of all Wycoller's bridges. Clam Bridge is formed of a simple slab thrown across the stream, a rudimentary measure that has nevertheless lasted for more than 1000 years.

In about 200m, look for a signposted path on the right; leave the track and follow this path as it heads for Turnhole Clough. The path follows the beck upwards, crossing it on a little wooden footbridge. Carry on along the opposite side of the beck through oak, beech and birchwoods to reach a kissing gate. Leave the wood and continue along its top edge, rising to rockier open ground, at its best in early autumn as the scatter of rowan trees blaze with pillar-box-red berries and leaves.

Pass through a gate to join a major track, the Pennine Bridleway. Turn left, signed for Wycoller, to cross New Bridge. This sturdy construction is evidence of

recent engineering investment in the route. Keep straight on along the bridleway, ignoring the turnings as you pass a crossroads. Shortly after, the bridleway joins a tarmac track and climbs slightly to a signpost. Turn left here, following both the Pennine Bridleway and the Pendle Way towards Wycoller, through a metal gate. The track descends alongside Smithy Clough, passing the farm at Parson Lee. As the path from Turnhole Clough rejoins from the left, you are back on the outward route. Return to Wycoller village and the car park, making time to visit the tearoom, paddle in the beck or hunt for ghosts!

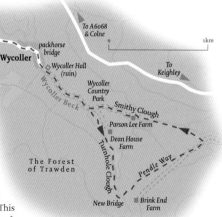

The wide valleys of the Aire and Wharfe mark the beginning of the transformation from the gritstone South Pennine hills to the limestone country of the Yorkshire Dales beyond. Both rivers begin in the Dales, meandering their way through the market towns of Skipton, Keighley and Ilkley to meet near Leeds. The valley of the Worth, flowing through Oxenhope and Haworth into the Aire at Keighley, is widely known as Brontë Country, after the famous family of authors. The literary-minded can find plenty of fascinating context for the Brontë sisters' work in the moorlands, valleys and weaving villages surrounding the area. More recent fame came with the 1970 film of *The Railway Children*, filmed along the Keighley and Worth Valley Steam Railway.

To the north, the area between the Aire and Wharfe Valleys is taken up by the mass of Rombald Moor. Rich in Neolithic evidence, there are several historic rock carvings to be found. The most famous area of the moor is around the spa town of Ilkley, immortalised in Yorkshire's 'national' anthem, 'On Ilkley Moor Baht'at'. Be sure to heed the song's warning of wandering on here 'baht'at' (without a hat)!

Brontë Country and Ilkley Moor

Valley of the Railway Children

**Distance 6.5km Time 2 hours 30
Terrain lanes and paths with one hill
Map OS Explorer OL21 Access buses (B3)
from Keighley and Hebden Bridge, and
steam trains along the Keighley and
Worth Valley Railway**

**One of Britain's best loved films, the 1970
production of *The Railway Children* was
filmed around the Keighley and Worth
Valley Railway. This circular walk visits
two of the stations on this standard
gauge heritage line, as well as passing
the fictional home of the children and
their mother. An ascent to nearby
Penistone Hill offers wide views across
the Worth Valley and the neighbouring
moors of Brontë Country.**

Start from the entrance to Oxenhope
Railway Station. Walk along Mill Lane, the
road between the station car park and the
Millennium Green. Cross the beck and
turn left by the relief car park, signed

Worth Way and Brontë Way. The path runs
alongside Bridgehouse Beck and soon
comes to a T-junction. Turn left, cross the
beck and on the far side keep straight
ahead up some steps and across the
railway (signed Brontë Way). Ascend the
side of the field, passing the house of
Bents at the top, the location for Three
Chimneys, the film home of the three
railway children and their mother. Jiggle
left, then right past the houses, staying
on the track.

At the end, turn left along Marsh Lane.
After 200m, turn right into Old Oxenhope
Lane. Where this lane turns 90 degrees
left, keep straight ahead through a
farmyard at the Public Footpath sign and
onto the rising path beyond. Enjoy views
across the Worth Valley and Keighley, but
be alert to the path soon swapping sides
of the wall. Coming to a tarmac driveway,
turn left and ascend to meet a road at the
top. Turn right and after 100m turn left

◄ Oxenhope Station

along a stone track, into the heather and bilberry dome of Penistone Hill. At the parking area, take a path bearing right and passing the level grassy floor of an old quarry. Follow this up to the right, around the top of the quarry, and watch for the trig point on the plateau ahead. There is a network of paths on the hill, which is designated as a country park, so you could take any number of alternatives.

At the trig point, this route turns right and descends to reach a junction with a fingerpost. Here, bear right, signed for Haworth. Cross a road and go straight ahead down a tarmac path, signed for Haworth village. At the bottom, turn left, also signed for Haworth, and walk along the paved path above the main Haworth car park area. This reaches Haworth Parish Church, with the famous Brontë Parsonage House set back beyond the graveyard to the left. This was the childhood home of the Brontë sisters, Anne, Charlotte and Emily, and is open to the public (charge). At the far side of the church, turn right and descend Haworth's photogenic cobbled main street, flanked by cafés, pubs and some quirky independent retailers. Opposite the Fleece Inn bear left to leave the main street. Cross a busy road with a useful zebra crossing and walk on down Butt Lane. At the bottom a bridge crosses the Keighley

and Worth Valley Railway to arrive at the front of Haworth Station.

Turn right along Station Road. At the mini-roundabout, keep straight ahead. In a few metres, the road bends sharply to the left. Just around the corner, find a footpath on the right, signed for Oxenhope. The path works its way along the valley just above the railway. Be careful to turn right immediately after passing the front of a house and remain with the footpath as it weaves along the wooded valley floor, close to Bridgeholme Beck. The final section retraces the outward path to Oxenhope Station.

Nab Hill

Distance 8km Time 2 hours 30
Terrain tracks and moorland paths
Map OS Explorer OL21 Access buses (B3)
from Keighley and Hebden Bridge, and
steam trains on the Keighley and Worth
Valley Railway

The mill village of Oxenhope marks
the end of the Worth Valley, the slopes
beyond rising to the bleak moors.
Overlooking the silenced mills and sooty
terraces is the craggy edge of Nab Hill,
a terrific viewpoint scattered with
hummocks and cairns. The walk along its
balcony-like rim rewards with excellent
views back to the valley below.

From the centre of Oxenhope, head
south along Station Road. Passing the big
mill chimney on your right, fork right into
Jew Lane. At a second fork, carry straight
on, following a Brontë Way marker down a
dead-end road. At the end, take the grassy
track and then cross a bridge over the
Leeming Water. Climb past a farmhouse,
then bear left on a public footpath to
arrive at a junction by Leeming Reservoir.

Follow the signposted Brontë Way to
Thornton, on the lane heading straight up
the hill. Shortly after, at a fork in the track,
bear left (avoiding the turn up to the
houses). As the lane bends round, leave it
to follow the signed Brontë Way on a path
slightly to your left. This narrow path
passes between hedges and across marshy
meadowland studded with flowers of
ragged robin in summer.

Climbing alongside Stony Hill, leave
the trees behind to pass through banks of
heather and bilberry, before emerging
into fields of rough pasture. Pass through
a gate and continue uphill. The path veers
round to the left onto the crest of the hill

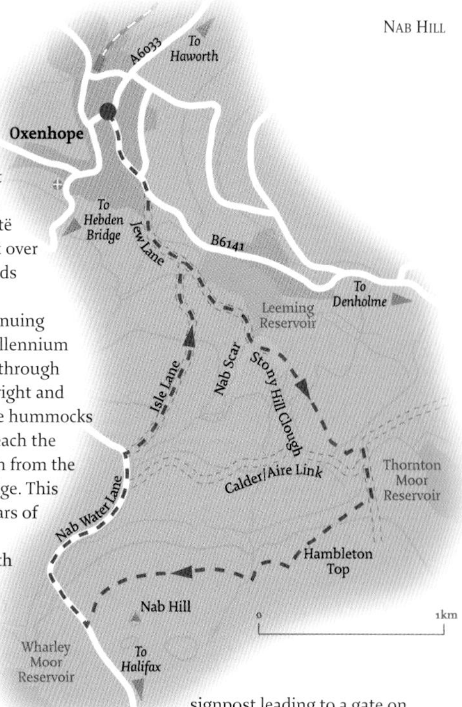

and heads up to a fingerpost marking a junction of paths. At this point, leave the Brontë Way, instead cutting straight over to join a cobbled track towards a metal barred gate.

Go through the gate, continuing slightly upwards. (signed Millennium Way, circular walk). Soon go through another metal gate on your right and climb diagonally towards the hummocks of Hambleton Top. As you reach the brow of the hill, join the path from the left, which runs along the edge. This is an area dotted with the scars of human activity; there are disused quarry workings, with leftover stones turned into a series of cairns by walkers. One of Simon Armitage's Stanza Stones, entitled *Mist*, may also be found here. Oxenhope and Haworth appear in the sweep of the Worth Valley below and Ovenden Moor Wind Farm can be seen to the south. The path continues weaving through the enigmatic delphs and quarries along the edge of Nab Hill.

Descend on the path to meet Nab Water Lane, opposite Warley Moor Reservoir. Turn right and follow the lane downhill. Ignore the first turning to the right, staying on the lane as it curves around the head of a valley. Just as the road veers sharp left, look for a 'restricted byway'

signpost leading to a gate on the right. Take this track, which follows the top of the valley side. Keep straight downhill on the track to reach a shallow wall cutting ending at a signpost. Turn left at the 'Isle Lane, restricted byway' sign.

Continue over a grassy area to the back of a row of houses, reaching another signpost for Isle Lane. Follow the lane and the signposts down the hill. Leeming Dam will appear on the right as you rejoin the outward route to Oxenhope, via Jew Lane and Station Road.

Brontë Bridge and Wuthering Heights

Distance 9km Time 2 hours 30
Terrain moorland paths and tracks, with
a return through a hilltop village
Map OS Explorer OL21 Access bus (B1-3)
from Keighley to nearby Haworth or
(B1, K16) to Stanbury

The term 'Brontë Country' refers to the
Pennine hills and moors that surround
Haworth, home of the three literary
sisters. They explored the hinterland of
Haworth over the years they lived in the
Parsonage House. Emily wrote only one
novel, *Wuthering Heights*, but its name has
become synonymous with the bleak and
wild setting for a story of exploitation
and cruelty.

The bedrock of millstone grit creates an
air of barren desolation and, though this
walk is not long, it has the atmosphere of
adventure. Crossing the Brontë Bridge, it
ascends onto windswept moors just
below the watershed with Calderdale.

Here is the lonely outpost of Top Withins,
perhaps the model for Wuthering Heights.

Penistone Hill Country Park straddles
the hillside just to the west of Haworth.
There is a car park by the summit of the
road between Oxenhope and Stanbury.
Cross the road to take a footpath
traversing the heather-clad moor. In
about 1km merge into a broad track
running alongside a wall with the solemn
profile of the high moorland looming
ahead. It becomes a footpath and
descends to cross South Dene Beck at
Brontë Bridge, allegedly one of the Brontë
sisters' favourite places. The present
structure only dates from 1990, replacing
an earlier crossing washed away by
floodwater. The Brontë waterfall lies a
short way upstream.

Cross the bridge and then grind uphill
on the footpath opposite, but it's not far
to a fingerpost where the left-hand fork is
signed to Top Withins. Stone flags aid

◀ Brontë Bridge

passage and the route soon levels out to follow the rim of the valley. The spectre of the ruins at Top Withins on the distant hillside beckons, guarded by two lonely trees. This is bleak and desolate moorland, covered with heather and bracken and founded on hard sandstone outcrops. Stepping stones cross the upper reaches of the beck before a final ascent to a junction with the Pennine Way, next to a ruined farmhouse.

Turn left here and continue a further 200m to reach Top Withins, customarily known as Wuthering Heights. Although the deserted farmhouse does not resemble the description in Emily Brontë's 1847 novel, the position and aura reflect its remote and austere location, so it has traditionally been seen as the imagined location of the classic story. Turn round and enjoy a panoramic view towards Haworth and way beyond.

From Top Withins, return on the Pennine Way but keep straight ahead at

the junction, remaining on the long-distance path. In 1.5km, after passing the house at Upper Heights, bear left, signed for Stanbury, with the path now becoming a roughly surfaced track. Soon the Pennine Way turns off to the left but keep ahead, continuing along the track and lane towards the village of Stanbury.

Stanbury straddles a spur of land on the moorland road between Haworth and Colne. It enjoys two pubs, the Friendly and the Wuthering Heights. Nearby Ponden Hall is also reputed to have literary links with the Brontës. Just after the end of the village, turn right, taking the road signed for Oxenhope. Cross the dam of Lower Laithe Reservoir with care as there is no footpath here. Climb up on the far side to return to Penistone Hill Country Park.

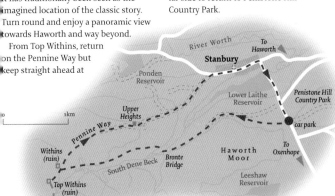

Keighley Moor and Newsholme Dean

**Distance 10km Time 2 hours 30
Terrain a mix of moorland, field and
woodland paths Map OS Explorer OL21
Access buses (various) from Keighley to
Stanbury or Oakworth**

**Built to serve local industry, Keighley
Moor Reservoir now supplies drinking
water from a remote hollow amidst a
sea of heather. An airy moorland stroll
reaches its isolated perch, just below
the Pennine watershed, while the route
through Newsholme Dean meanders
by a sheltered green valley.**

There is a parking area by an old quarry
on Harehills Lane, the road between
Oakworth and Colne, about 4km west of
Oakworth and 500m west of the Grouse
Inn. A footpath rises from the back of the
car park to meet a track running along the
top of the quarry. Follow this to the right
through some other old workings,
bearing right at a gateway by a marker for
the Millennium Way. Soon arrive on open
moors and enjoy extensive views

northwards to the Yorkshire Dales with
the distinctive crouching profile of
Pen-y-ghent on the horizon. In 300m
there is a crossing of paths next to a pole.
Turn left here to cross the moor on the
signed Millennium Way.

The path leads all the way to Keighley
Moor Reservoir, 2km ahead, at first next
to a wall, later swapping sides. Some side-
stepping is needed to avoid some boggy
sections but there are no serious
difficulties. Heather spreads to the far
horizons, offering free range to the red
grouse. Leaving the wall, continue across
open moor, rising slightly to reach the
dam wall of Keighley Moor Reservoir.
Cross the dam wall to the right. At the far
side, turn right and follow the reservoir
access road downhill, alongside the valley
of Morkin Beck. This reaches the road at
Morkin Bridge, an alternative car park and
start to the walk.

Turn left and walk up the road for
200m. Turn right to follow a public right
of way through the gateway to

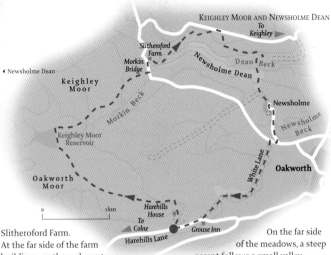

Newsholme Dean

Slitheroford Farm

Morkin Bridge

Keighley Moor

Morkin Beck

Keighley Moor Reservoir

Oakworth Moor

Harehills House

To Colne

Harehills Lane

Grouse Inn

Newsholme Dean

Dean Beck

Newsholme

Newsholme Beck

White Lane

Oakworth

To Keighley

0   1km

Slitheroford Farm.
At the far side of the farm buildings, go through a gate and turn right, down a field, to reach the beck. Follow this through a lovely riverside meadow before fording a small side stream and climbing a steep bank. The path continues through fields linked by stiles, above the valley. It rounds the side of a steep wooded clough, passes a barn and reaches a concrete driveway. Follow this up to the road. Turn right but in just 50m leave the road to turn right onto the signed public bridleway. A fine walled track trends downhill amongst bilberry, overlooking the attractive valley of Newsholme Dean. Sidle into another track a little further on, coming to a gate. Turn sharp right just in front of the gate, next to a stone shed (bridleway marker post). Drop around the grounds of some houses to arrive at the bottom of the valley. A footbridge and adjacent peculiar clapper bridge cross the beck.

On the far side of the meadows, a steep ascent follows a small valley through old woodland, with birch, holly, willow and mountain ash among the varied species. At the top, go through a gate and follow a fenced field-side footpath with views over Keighley. Shortly come to a walled track on a bend and carry straight on, heading for the houses. On entering the hamlet of Newsholme, bear right and the track soon becomes a tarmac lane leading downhill to cross Newsholme Beck. Beyond this it ascends to meet a road. Turn right and shortly turn left into White Lane which soon becomes a walled track. After a slight descent, curve right at a junction, staying on the track along the edge of woodland. At a bend look for the Second World War memorial at the site of a Canadian plane crash. Emerge onto a road opposite the Grouse Inn and follow this to the right, soon arriving back at the start.

The Pinnacles of Earl Crag

Distance 10km **Time** 2 hours 30
Terrain good tracks and field paths; two
ascents **Map** OS Explorer OL21 **Access** bus
(M4) from Keighley and Burnley

**Two towers crown the rocks of Earl Crag:
Lund's Tower and Wainman's Pinnacle.
The walk from Cowling passes through
lovely waterside meadows before rising
over the fields to an airy promenade
along the edge of the crag. Quiet tracks
explore the hillside and return through
the pretty hamlet of Ickornshaw.**

There is some road parking in Cowling
near the parish church, at the start of the
walk. Take the track to the right-hand side
of the graveyard, straddling a ridge above
the Ickornshaw Beck. After a barn, the
bridleway becomes a hedged lane and
later, just past Wood House, joins the
beck to provide an attractive promenade.
You soon cross the chasm of Gill Beck on
the high-level Ridge Mill Bridge. A plaque
records its construction in 2011 as a
replacement for an earlier crossing. On the
far side, turn right and enjoy a sequence
of pleasant waterside meadows. Watch
out for some steps down through the
trees, which bring you to Lane
Ends Bridge.

On the far side turn left and walk along
the lane, soon re-crossing the beck and
then rising to meet another road. Turn
right and walk along the road for about
800m to reach the main A6068. Turn left
along the pavement for about 200m, then
cross the road and turn right up the 'no-
through road' to High Malsis Farm. Pass
farm buildings and a row of houses to
reach the road end. Bear right at the sign
for Lund's Tower, through a small stile
and up the track beyond. There is now a
steady, direct climb up several fields
towards the craggy escarpment ahead.
Eventually pass to the right of an
abandoned farm and reach a gate onto
the road.

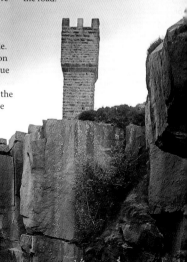

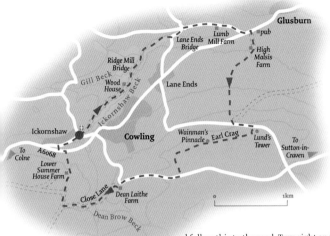

Turn left towards Lund's Tower. Just below it, leave the road, turning sharp right along a public footpath, signed for Cowling Pinnacle. This rises to the right of sandstone crags to reach the Tower, also known as Sutton Pinnacle. Built in 1887 by textile manufacturer James Lund, opinions differ about his motivation. Was it to celebrate Queen Victoria's jubilee or, more personally, to mark the birth of his daughter? Return along the path, keeping straight ahead along the top of the escarpment until you arrive at the second Victorian edifice, Wainman's (or Cowling) Pinnacle. Erected in 1898, it was a rather delayed commemoration of the Napoleonic Wars nearly a century before.

After enjoying the view keep straight on past the monument for another 300m before coming to a tarmac lane. Turn left and follow this to the road. Turn right and walk along the road for about 800m to where it bends sharply to the right. Keep straight ahead here and follow the track, Close Lane, as it drops into the peaceful valley of Dean Brow Beck. Ford the water and ascend the bridleway on the far side, accompanied by a small stream and a row of alder trees. A stiff pull reaches some meadows and then a junction with the long-distance footpath, the Pennine Way.

Turn right along the Way, keeping ahead past a barn and down a walled lane. The footpath diverts around the buildings at Lower Summer House Farm and on down a meadow to the main road at Ickornshaw. Cross the road, turning left along the footpath for a short distance. Just past a bus shelter, turn right to find a narrow path descending to a minor road. Turn right and walk through the village to Cowling Parish Church.

◀ Lund's Tower   **69**

Pinhaw Beacon and Lothersdale

Distance 5km **Time** 1 hour 30
Terrain field and moorland paths with
one steady ascent **Map** OS Explorer OL21
Access no regular public transport to
the start

Pinhaw Beacon commands a lofty
vantage point, the terminal outpost
of the gritty South Pennine uplands.
Its strategic location was the reason for
its title as a lookout point during the
Napoleonic Wars. At its foot, the
community of Lothersdale snakes along
an attractive pastoral valley crossed by
the Pennine Way. A circular walk uses
field paths to reach the summit of the
Beacon and crosses the heather moors
that spread over its top. Be aware that
dogs are not allowed on the open
moorland section.

Lothersdale is tucked away in a fold of
hills between Skipton and Colne, reached
by roads from these two towns and from
neighbouring Cross Hills. From the Hare

and Hounds in the village, walk west
about 200m to the junction with Side Gate
Lane. Just past this, opposite no 4 North
View, watch out for a small stile in the
wall. This leads to an old dam wall and a
footbridge beyond. Ascend the right-hand
side of the next small field, crossing a
further field with a stone barn to your
right. The right of way rises steeply along
the side of the next field. On reaching the
brow of the hill, trend left, aiming for the
buildings at Knott Barn ahead. Pass
through a gap in the wall and a gate
before following a track, then round the
side of the buildings to meet the road.

Turn left along the road for 200m, then
bear right on a concrete driveway at a
Public Footpath sign. Where this levels
out on a shoulder, the track forks. Take
the left-hand option, the driveway for Calf
Edge Farm. Just before reaching the

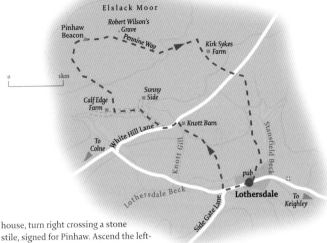

house, turn right crossing a stone stile, signed for Pinhaw. Ascend the left-hand side of the field, aiming for a gate and stile in the top corner. The next slope is tackled diagonally, with a marker-post indicating the way halfway up, then aiming for the upper edge of a plantation at the top. Pass through a gate, then almost immediately bear right, crossing a couple of stiles onto open moorland. A squelchy path goes ahead to meet a track. Turn right up this to conquer the summit of Pinhaw Beacon, marked by a trig point and stone cairn.

This height marks the northern extremity of the South Pennines, with views ahead across the Aire Gap, a wide breach in the succession of uplands that stretch up the watershed of Northern England, collectively known as the Pennines. North of the Gap the limestone heights of the Yorkshire Dales are ranged across the horizon. The commanding view

explains why this was the site of a beacon during the Napoleonic Wars. From the summit follow the track, now the Pennine Way, as it traverses the broad crest of the moor between wide swards of heather. Notice a side path to the left which leads to the site of Robert Wilson's grave. He was the chief beacon keeper but died during severe weather in 1805. He has since been buried in nearby Elslack churchyard.

Leaving the moors, stay on the Pennine Way, dropping down through some fields and joining a concrete farm track to a road. Cross the road and descend the next field. Immediately after the next stile, the Pennine Way turns right, following a wall. Stay with the long-distance footpath down fields and along a track until it returns to Lothersdale.

On Ilkley Moor

Distance 8km **Time** 2 hours 30
Terrain a mixture of sandy paths, steep in places, flagstone paths and rough lanes
Map OS Explorer 297 **Access** trains from Leeds and Bradford to Ilkley, and regular buses to the town

Ilkley Moor is the most northerly part of the sweeping Rombald's Moor. Its close proximity to Ilkley town, not to mention its immortalisation in the song 'On Ilkley Moor Baht'at', has also made it the best known area. This walk passes remnants of Ilkley's past as a spa town, as well as medieval and Neolithic remains on the wilder moorland above, accompanied by sweeping views of Wharfedale.

From the centre of Ilkley, walk up Wells Promenade. This wide street of Victorian villas is a relic of Ilkley's spa-town heritage, as is the small wooded park in the centre of the road. Follow the path through here, alongside a small stream,

to reach the top of Wells Promenade. Just before the road crosses a cattle grid, bear left to a gate with a signpost. Go through the gate and head straight ahead up a stepped path, passing an ornamental pond on the right and a small pavilion on the left. Follow the path, heading for a conspicuous white building on the hillside ahead of you.

This is the former bath house of White Wells, built by a Squire Middleton in the 18th century. Popular with Victorian tourists, the baths later fell into disuse, but were restored in the 1970s. They now act as a café, open on weekends and when a flag is flying outside.

Head behind the building to the right, finding a footpath reaching uphill, signed as the Millennium Way. This wide gravel path leads diagonally up the hillside below a clump of wind-weathered pine trees. Looking back, enjoy wide-ranging views over Ilkley and the Wharfe Valley.

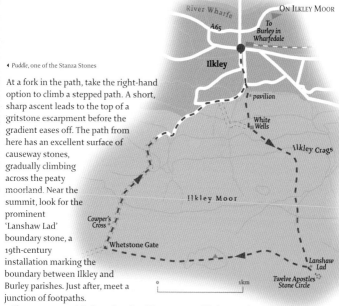

◄ Puddle, one of the Stanza Stones

At a fork in the path, take the right-hand option to climb a stepped path. A short, sharp ascent leads to the top of a gritstone escarpment before the gradient eases off. The path from here has an excellent surface of causeway stones, gradually climbing across the peaty moorland. Near the summit, look for the prominent 'Lanshaw Lad' boundary stone, a 19th-century installation marking the boundary between Ilkley and Burley parishes. Just after, meet a junction of footpaths.

The route turns right here, but first it's worth a quick deviation to visit the Twelve Apostles Stone Circle. To do so, carry on to the left for 100m to find the ring of small stones. These have been here much longer than Lanshaw Lad: since the Bronze Age! There are theories that the circle formed a kind of druidical sun dial, but as with all Neolithic remains, an air of compelling mystery hangs over the scene.

Having concluded your audience with the Apostles, retrace your steps back to the junction of paths. This time go left to pass Lanshaw Lad, then cross the moor on another path of causeway stones. Pass a trig point on the right and, just before the path meets a wall, look for the *Puddle*

stone. This is one of a trail of Stanza Stones, linking Ilkley with Marsden, near Huddersfield; each has a carved poem by Pennine poet, Simon Armitage. Continue along the edge of the wall, past a radio mast, to a junction with a road end. Turn right along the rough potholed track, passing near Cowper's Cross just to the left of the path. This is another of Ilkley Moor's antiquities, thought to date from the 12th century. Who knows what led to it being erected in this lonely spot? Shortly after the cross, the track begins to descend and Ilkley reappears below. Continue to walk downhill as the track joins a road, returning to the top of Wells Promenade and Ilkley town centre.

73

Cow and Calf

Distance 5km **Time** 1 hour 30
Terrain mixture of sandy paths, steep in
places, with tarmac tracks
Map OS Explorer 297 **Access** trains
from Leeds and Bradford to Ilkley, and
regular buses to the town

The edges of Ilkley Moor have been a
popular playground since Victorian
times, as local people came to visit the
bath houses, ice skate and take in the
views over the Wharfe Valley. One of the
most notable landmarks is Hangingstone
Rocks, a combination of a large gritstone
outcrop and smaller boulder known
colloquially as 'Cow and Calf'. This short
circuit from Ilkley visits the rocks and
other traditional tourist attractions on
Ilkley Moor.

From the centre of Ilkley, walk up Wells
Promenade, a wide Victorian street
embellished with trees and a tumbling
stream. Climb the road to reach a cattle
grid; just before crossing it, bear left to a
gate with a signpost. Follow the signpost
to the left, along a tarmac track.

Shortly afterwards, you arrive at Ilkley
Tarn. This small ornamental lake is a
legacy of the Victorians' development of
Ilkley as a recreational area. This edge of
the moor was particularly popular with
Sunday School visitors, especially in
winter, when the tarn froze and became a
popular ice-skating venue. The most
famous legacy of the Sunday School
visitors is the song, 'On Ilkley Moor
Bah'tat'. Local children took a long-
forgotten tune for the Christmas carol
'While Shepherds Watched their Flocks'
and revamped it with a new set of words
about a pair of lovers on the moor. The
song illustrates the perils of being
'bahtat' (without a hat) on the moor, as
the lover catches a chill and dies, his body
then feasted on by worms. You have been
warned; put on suitable headgear before
travelling any further!

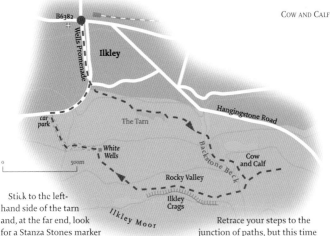

Stick to the left-hand side of the tarn and, at the far end, look for a Stanza Stones marker post. Take the path just to the left of this, crossing the hillside. Descend to cross the tumbling, pine tree-hooded ravine of Backstone Beck on a small footbridge. Immediately afterwards, the main path veers left, but instead look for another Stanza Stones marker on the right, and take the narrow path climbing steeply from here alongside the beck.

Reaching the top of the ravine, come to a T-junction. Turn left to visit the Cow and Calf rocks, with its excellent views back over Wharfedale. Local legend has it that the Calf was split from the Cow by the giant Rombald. Fleeing from his angry wife, he stamped on the rock as he leapt across the valley. This legend also encompasses another local landmark; the giant's wife is said to have dropped the stones held in her skirt, creating a nearby rock formation, The Skirtful of Stones. There is a café at the Cow and Calf car park below if you require refreshments.

Retrace your steps to the junction of paths, but this time continue straight ahead. Shortly after, cross the tumbling, rum-dark headwaters of Backstone Beck.

Continue on the path below the craggy escarpment on your left, taking the lower of two options to lead you down into Rocky Valley. This unimaginatively named groove between dramatic crags is popular with climbers. Descend on the path to the 18th-century bath house at White Wells, where a plaque commemorates the Moor's famous song. There is another option for refreshments at the tearooms here, open on weekends and whenever a flag is flying.

Walk behind the building to take the broad track leading to the west of a compass fingerpost. This descends gently, curving over a beck by a small waterfall, and leads down to White Wells car park. Turn right on the road from here to head back down to Wells Promenade and Ilkley town centre.

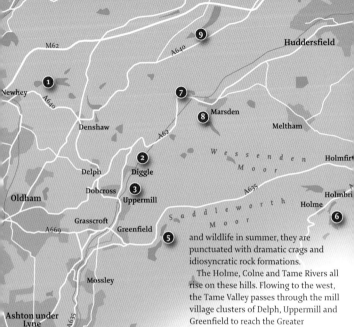

This is the most southerly part of the region covered in this volume, where the counties of Greater Manchester, West Yorkshire and Derbyshire converge on the vast sweep of Saddleworth and Wessenden Moors. These are the northernmost reaches of the Peak District National Park, named the Dark Peak after their chiselled gritstone and acidic peat soils. The moors here can be bleak and lonely, but contain some of our most beautiful wilderness; alive with colour and wildlife in summer, they are punctuated with dramatic crags and idiosyncratic rock formations.

The Holme, Colne and Tame Rivers all rise on these hills. Flowing to the west, the Tame Valley passes through the mill village clusters of Delph, Uppermill and Greenfield to reach the Greater Manchester Conurbation. On the Yorkshire side of the watershed, the Colne rises above Marsden and the Holme above Holmfirth, both flowing towards Huddersfield. Their valleys pass from moorland to green rolling hills of drystone walls and pasture, with sooty mill cottages clustered below. The gentler landscape of these lower hills and valleys has been immortalised in long-running sitcom 'The Last of the Summer Wine', which has spawned something of a cottage industry in Holmfirth, especially. In common with the other settlements around here, you'll never be short of a good teashop after your walk!

Summer Wine and Saddleworth

Piethorne Valley

**Distance 6km Time 1 hour 30
Terrain reservoir access tracks and
good footpaths Map OS Explorer OL21
Access bus (451) from Rochdale to the
end of the road; more buses and
Metrolink trams from nearby Newhey**

The Piethorne Valley is one of those
beauty spots which is very popular with
local communities but unlikely to be
known by those from further afield.
The valley's intriguing name has nothing
to do with baked goods: *pie* is an old
English word for 'magpies' while *thorne*
may refer to the wizened hawthorn trees
scattered across the valley. To this day,
the nature-conscious walker may spot
both of these during this pleasant
exploration of the valley's reservoirs,
woodland and moorland fringes.

Start from Piethorne car park on
Waterworks Road, Ogden. There are public
toilets and a local ranger office here. Take
the signposted footpath almost exactly
opposite the ranger office, which climbs
uphill through a field before emerging
onto a quiet lane. Follow the lane uphill
to the left and continue upwards as the
cobbled track weaves between the
buildings of Manor House Farm and
Oakdene. Keep ascending, ignoring a
private turn-off to the right. At the crest of
the hill, the track is lined with bilberry
bushes, attracting bees, butterflies and
moths in summer.

As the track levels off, Denshaw village
and the valleys of Saddleworth appear
beyond. Here, the track forks; bear left.
Keeping Edge Gate Farm and its stables on
your right, continue straight ahead to find
a gate at the end of the farmyard.
Continue your trajectory on the moorland
path beyond the gate, following the wall
as Rooden Reservoir comes into view.
Rooden is home to oystercatchers and
other wading birds in summer; listen
out for their keening calls drifting
through the air.

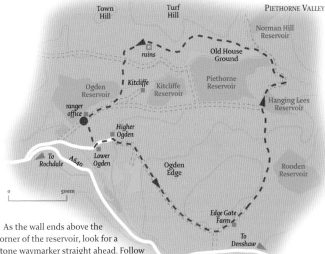

As the wall ends above the corner of the reservoir, look for a stone waymarker straight ahead. Follow the series of waymarkers along the grassy path heading down into the Piethorne Valley, ultimately reaching a stile. Below on the left there are now good views to Piethorne Reservoir; on the right is the much smaller Hanging Lees Reservoir, constructed in 1870 to intercept silt washed down from the moors.

Cross the stile to join the reservoir access road, continuing across Hanging Lees Dam. The track passes among a few lonely birch and hawthorn trees before arriving at a crossing of tracks. Take the sharp left downhill. Rounding the head of Piethorne Reservoir, pass the small building of Lime House and the outflow from Norman Hill Reservoir on your right. The track begins to climb again, passing behind some trees. Just before a gate, there is a gap in the wall to the left. Take the path through this gap, passing a sign

for Old House Ground. This is the official name of the beech and pine plantation here; local parlance has it, much more idyllically, as Bluebell Wood.

Walk through this peaceful grove of twisted trees, emerging on the side of the hill. The path ambles around the curves of the valley side, passing the stone ruins of the 13th-century Binns Farm. Eventually, near the top end of Ogden Reservoir, the path joins a track. Looking slightly to the left, you will see a stile and a waymarker post. Cross the stile to follow this path downhill through a series of fields to reach a small footbridge over the inlet of the reservoir. Cross the bridge and climb again, with the wall on your right, to join another rising track. As this meets a lane, turn right, passing some cottages to return to the car park.

Romans and Victorians

Distance 11km **Time** 3 hours
Terrain mainly good tracks and quiet
lanes **Map** OS Explorer OL21 **Access** buses
(180) from Oldham and Huddersfield
and (354) from Ashton to Uppermill

Roman roads, turnpikes, canals and
railways have all funnelled their way
across the moors of Standedge, some
above ground and some beneath it. This
route around Diggle passes Roman forts,
Georgian canals and Victorian reservoirs
and railways, with a panoramic ascent of
Harrop Edge and Brun Clough.

Begin at Brownhill Countryside Centre
on the northern edge of Uppermill.
Leaving the car park, turn left and cross
the canal on Dobcross New Road. Shortly
afterwards, cross the road to turn down
Nicker Brow. The signed public footpath
leads between hedges to begin a stiff
climb up the hill; continue straight
upwards as the path turns into a track,
merging with a minor road as you enter
Dobcross village. Amidst the charming

cottages of Dob Cross Square, turn right
at The Swan pub to take Sandy Lane
uphill. After about 200m, bear left up
Long Lane.

Leaving the village behind, the lane
reverts to a rough track as it rises. Follow
this as it curves left and passes Lark Hill
farmhouse to a crossing of tracks. Straight
ahead are wonderful views into the valley
of Delph, but our route turns right, along
Harrop Edge. For the next 1.5km enjoy the
views across the valley on the gentle
traverse of the ridge. Just in front of a
small conifer plantation, turn left down a
track to reach the Saddleworth Hotel.
Cross the road and turn left for a short
distance to a signposted footpath.
Crossing the stile, take this path through
the meadows to meet another lane and
turn right. Shortly after this, pass the
entrance to Castle Shaw car park; a short
diversion through here enables you to
access interpretation boards about the
reservoirs and the Roman fort nearby.

Exiting the car park through a gate, turn

◄ Dobcross

left along Cote Lane and take the first kissing gate on your right. Now follow the grassy path uphill past a marker post and enter the gated area of the old Roman fort. This lonely outpost dates from around 79AD and guarded the York to Chester road from rebellious Britons.

Leave the fort by a stile at the top end. Turn right along Bleak Hey Nook Lane, which winds its way up past farmhouses to a T-junction. Turn left here, then immediately left again, through a gate, to join a walled track. Heading uphill, the track runs parallel to the lane and eventually rejoins it. Where the lane forks down to the right, continue upwards on the rocky track of the Pennine Bridleway. Just after cresting the brow of the hill, turn right to follow the bridleway, with Brun Clough Reservoir now in your sights.

Cross the A62 and take the track opposite, meandering down past Keeper's Cottage, its summers haunted by the cries of lapwing. Follow the marker posts for the Pennine Bridleway downhill along the track, passing Diggle Edge Farm, and continue down to the Diggle Hotel. Turn right over the railway bridge, then follow the road round to the left. At the next bend, turn into the car park and walk through it to join the canal towpath by the Standedge Tunnel portal. Construction of the tunnel, the longest and highest of its kind in Britain, was not easy. It took the expertise of Thomas Telford to notice a severe misalignment, saving the project great expense. The tunnel finally opened in 1811 but was soon superseded by the Leeds to Manchester Railway. The frequent rumble of trains on this busy transPennine route remind us that Diggle remains an important transport corridor.

Continue on the towpath past a series of locks. At Lock 25, the towpath peters out. Cross the small footbridge here and continue on the other side of the canal. Just after Bridge 73, exit to Brownhill Countryside Centre on your left. There's a café here and in nearby Uppermill.

81

Pots and Pans

Distance 7km **Time** 2 hours
Terrain quiet lanes, bridleways and grassy
footpaths; some muddy and some have
steep sections **Map** OS Explorer OL1
Access buses from Oldham, Manchester
and Huddersfield to Uppermill

**The war memorial and curious rock
features of Pots and Pans dominate the
skyline above Saddleworth. This ascent
from the charming village of Uppermill
also allows a wider exploration of the
hillsides, through fields and rock-
scattered moors, with terrific views
across the North West.**

From Uppermill, take Station Road out
of the village centre. Just before passing
under a wooden bridge, ascend a flight of
railway sleeper steps on the right-hand
side to join the Pennine Bridleway. Turn
left along the track, an old railway line,
signed for Diggle.

Follow the tree-lined railway
embankment, veering slightly left at a
junction to continue on the bridleway.

Eventually, it begins rising up to a lane,
marking the point where a tunnel has
been filled in.

Turn right on the lane, then
immediately veer right again, passing
through a metal gate onto a track. Follow
the hedgeline as the track becomes a
path, continuing straight ahead at a
junction. Cross a beck and continue
upwards to a junction next to a pond.
Take the path on the right to reach a lane
and turn right, passing St Chad's Church
in the small hamlet of Pobgreen. Take the
footpath to the left, which runs around
the graveyard, then joins a track through
Ivy Bank Farm.

Reaching a T-junction, cross straight
over the road and a stile, waymarked
'Oldham Way'. This grassy path climbs
stiffly, following a well-worn groove
between dilapidated walls. Cross another
stile to join a walled track, continuing
your climb. The derelict ruins of Slades
Barn farm soon become visible to your
left. As you become level with the farm,

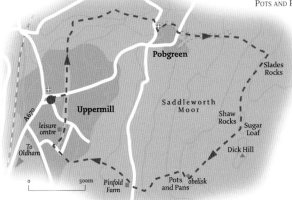

leave the track where it bends to the left. Instead, head for Slades Rocks, directly ahead. Aiming slightly to the right of a ruined drystone wall, ascend a grassy path to reach a marker post on the crest of the hill, just to the left of the rocks.

Turn right along the well-trodden path heading above the rocks, along the rim of Saddleworth Moor. There are great views from here. Cross a rudimentary stile to reach the jagged Shaw Rocks and a fork in the path. The left fork leads past Sugar Loaf, a lone boulder, but instead take the right-hand option. Shortly afterwards, join a track from the left and head for the obelisk at Pots and Pans.

Pass through a gate to reach the obelisk, a war memorial which hosts a hilltop memorial service every Remembrance Sunday. The name Pots and Pans refers not to the obelisk, but to the misshapen rocks to its left on which acid rain and waves of climbers have over many years worn hollows that collect water. The rocks provide the foreground to a vista that

seems to encompass the entire North West of England. On a clear day, you may even see North Wales.

Take the obvious grassy path heading straight downhill between the memorial and the rocks; descend steeply to reach a gate and follow the walled path beyond to meet a lane. Cross this to pass through the buildings of Pinfold Farm and then continue downhill through fields, with Uppermill in your sights below. Cross a series of stiles and a farm track to hold your course downhill to the bottom of the fields, exiting between leylandii hedges onto the tarmac lane of Ball Grove. At a junction, take Rush Hill Road ahead and pass over the old railway bridge; just afterwards, take the path on the right to join the old railway line. Turn left on the trackbed, passing Saddleworth Pool and Leisure Centre and crossing its car park. Continue on the Pennine Bridleway until just before the wooden bridge. Exit here by your outward route, signed for Uppermill village centre, along Station Road.

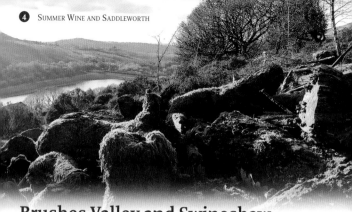

Brushes Valley and Swineshaw

Distance 7.5km Time 2 hours 30
Terrain a smorgasbord of surfaces,
from tarmac lanes to rocky tracks and
steep sandy paths. Wear boots!
Map OS Explorer OL1 Access regular buses
pass the country park entrance

East of Stalybridge, the Brushes Valley is
a mosaic of woodland, fields and
reservoirs set between Harridge Pike and
Wild Hill, the highest point in Tameside.
Dipping in and out of the valley before
rising to the Swineshaw Reservoirs at its
head, this walk offers great views back to
Manchester and Cheshire beyond.

Start at Oakgates car park. Go through
the metal gate and turn right on a wide
gravel track, signed for Walkerwood.
Climb to the top of the track and head out
of a gate to turn right onto a road.
Immediately after, cross a stile on the left,
just before houses.

Take the right-hand of two grassy paths,
climbing straight up the field. Exit

through a gap stile, turning left on a lane
to pass a farm and stables. Just after, look
for a signpost on the left, indicating a
narrow path jack-knifing back around the
farm. Follow this into the ruins of an old
rifle range amidst heather. Reach a
junction of paths and turn to the left.
Shortly after, at another junction, ignore a
waymarker pointing ahead; instead turn
right to walk in front of the fenceline.
Climb slightly past more ruins to go
through a gate and reach a T-junction.
Turn left on the path around the hillside,
with Walkerwood Reservoir now visible
below and Harridge Pike behind. At a fork,
veer left to go downhill towards the trees
below. The path descends steeply, bearing
scars of mountain bike activity; be vigilant
for the sound of tyres behind you!

The gradient eases as the path descends
into Cock Wood, an enchanted little forest
of gnarly oaks and pines in curious claw-
like shapes. Join a track from the left to
continue around the head of Walkerwood

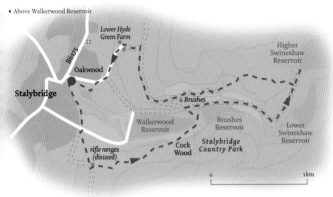

◀ Above Walkerwood Reservoir

Reservoir before climbing to a crossroads.

Turn right on the signed Pennine Bridleway for Tintwistle, along the tarmac waterboard road, climbing above Brushes Reservoir through banks of rhododendron. The road becomes steeper as it passes through oak woodland before emerging onto open moorland at the head of the valley. Passing Lower Swineshaw Reservoir on your right, the mass of Arnfield Moor appears ahead. This was the epicentre of the disastrous Saddleworth Moor Fire of June 2018, which blazed for three weeks and is estimated to have long-lasting impacts on moorland wildlife; a reminder that the moors, while bleak, are also a fragile environment.

Just before passing under powerlines, look for a gate and ladder stile on your left. Our route will continue this way, but first it's worth continuing 100m along the road to Higher Swineshaw Reservoir, a good picnic spot. Retrace your steps to the gate and follow the track over the moors as it weaves beneath powerlines.

As the track descends into the cleft of Harridge, Manchester and the Cheshire Plain now appear, with views to North Wales on clear days. The line of pylons is a bit of a distraction, but still preferable to the thick industrial smog that once precluded any views from here!

Continue to a junction with the Pennine Bridleway track. Turn right, following the bridleway until you pass through a metal gate and reach a junction with a rough lane, next to a signpost. Turn sharp left here to descend the lane through a series of small farms. At a T-junction at Lower Hyde Green Farm, turn left on Besom Lane. Just as you reach the built-up area, pass through a gate on the left next to a noticeboard for Stalybridge Country Park. Take this path, and shortly afterwards turn right on another path to pass a millpond. Cross through Besom Lane car park and take the path from the bottom, signed for Oakgates, to return to the start.

SUMMER WINE AND SADDLEWORTH

Dove Stone

Distance 12km Time 3 hours 30 (shorter option also available) Terrain exposed, rough moorland, rocky underfoot Map OS Explorer OL1 Access buses (180, 350) from Manchester, Oldham and Ashton to Waterside, 1km from the start

The moors around Saddleworth have a lingering dark reputation but provide scenery of stark and dramatic beauty. In the valley below sits Dove Stone Reservoir, framed by steeply rising gritstone crags topped with compelling and curious rock formations. Walking along the rim of the crags offers panoramic views over the valley and Greater Manchester.

Constructed in the 1960s by the Ashton, Stalybridge & Dukinfield Water Company, Dove Stone Reservoir is now a popular local beauty spot. Both the RSPB and Peak District National Park maintain offices here. The main car park (pay and

display) is at the foot of the reservoir dam, and there are toilets here. From this car park, follow the signposted track to Chew Reservoir, the highest reservoir in England when constructed in 1912. The vehicular track passes the sailing club and crosses a stream before heading uphill. Climbing steeply, the track clings to the side of a ravine littered with gritstone boulders.

On rounding a curve in the ravine, Chew dam wall appears in front of you. At this point, look for a small disused quarry. Just after passing this, ascend the grassy bank on the left-hand side of the track to join a sandy path running around the top of the quarry. This path follows the gritstone edge, with views across to the stegosaur-like rock formation of Wimberry Stones, known colloquially as 'Indian's Head', and to Greenfield beyond. The rocky crags in this area are an ideal home for peregrine falcons.

◀ Dove Stone

Continuing along the edge, the path passes Bramley's Cot, a ruined shooting lodge built into the rock. Heading towards Cairn on Fox Stone, views open up across the reservoir and over to Oldham and Manchester. From the cairn, the path veers right, following the edge. Passing above the dramatic cliffs at Dean Rocks, it then weaves around the head of the deep cleft above Ashway Gap, crossing several small becks. Some care is needed on these sections; there are a few boggy areas and also a couple of short scrambles.

After crossing the Ashway Gap, the route begins to descend, with Yeoman Hey Reservoir now visible in the valley beneath. Below the weathered pancake-stack of Ashway Stone, the path forks. Take the main path here, heading left downhill towards the reservoir. Visible up on the rocks to the right is the Ashworth Cross, a memorial to James Platt, MP for Oldham, killed in a shooting accident in 1857. Continue following the grassy path as it descends steeply down towards the upper end of Dove Stone Reservoir. At the bottom of the hill, join the circular reservoir track. There is also a picnic site here on the site of Ashway House, ideal for refuelling before the final stretch.

There is now a choice of routes back to the start point, both options following the edge of the reservoir. Turning left will take you on the more direct route, returning via the sailing club to the car park. A right turn will take you on a slightly longer route across Yeoman Hey dam and through the plantations on the other side of Dove Stone, finally returning across the lower dam to the car park.

A shorter and easier 5km walk option from the car park is to enjoy the circular walk around the reservoir. This is a well-signposted wheelchair-friendly trail, offering great views across the water and up to the rocky edges.

Head of the Holme Valley

Distance 7.5km Time 2 hours
Terrain field and reservoir paths, some
may be muddy Map OS Explorer OL21
Access bus (314) from Huddersfield to
Holmbridge or Holme

The Upper Holme Valley opens up from
mill villages to wooded cloughs and
finally onto the wild peaty hills that
make up the Peak District's northern
extremities. Overlooked by the imposing
Holme Moss transmission mast, the
hillsides offer far-reaching views over
South Kirklees. Meanwhile, nestling in
the valleys are a series of reservoirs and
hamlets, evidence of man's struggle to
forge a living through agriculture and
industry on these lonely hills.

Start from the car park at Ramsden
Reservoir. Reach this by turning off the
A6024 Holmfirth to Woodhead road at
Holmbridge. Walk a short way back along

the road before turning sharp left to take
the public footpath just below the dam.
At the far side the path turns right and
rises through natural oak woodland
around the side of the hill. Descend to
cross a small beck next to a picturesque
waterfall, turning sharp right and
ascending to the end of the wood.
Continue up the field and along a fenced
path to reach the main road in Holme.
The ancient settlement was destroyed by
William the Conqueror as a punishment
for rebellion, but today's village straddles
the main road in the lee of the Dark Peak.
It's the first and last village in Yorkshire
coming this way.

Turn left along the main road for 200m,
then turn right by the bus stop into Meal
Hill Road. After 200m leave this road to
take the Kirklees Way footpath. Soon, at
the end of the walled section, bear right
across the field to follow the public

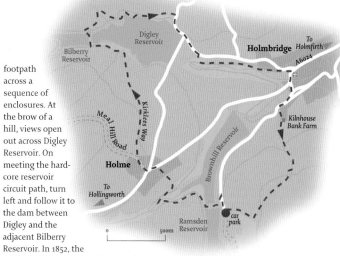

Digley
Reservoir

Bilberry
Reservoir

Holmbridge
To Holmfirth
A6024

Kirklees Way

Meal Hill Road

Holme

To
Hollingworth

Kilnhouse
Bank Farm

Brownhill Reservoir

Ramsden
Reservoir

car
park

0   500m

footpath across a sequence of enclosures. At the brow of a hill, views open out across Digley Reservoir. On meeting the hard-core reservoir circuit path, turn left and follow it to the dam between Digley and the adjacent Bilberry Reservoir. In 1852, the original Bilberry dam wall collapsed, unleashing a great flood which engulfed Holmbridge and Holmfirth. Once across its more stable replacement, zigzag up the hill on the perimeter path which winds through trees above the reservoir.

By the car park, just before arriving at the road, turn right, go down a flight of steps and follow the footpath to join the road a little further along. Turn right and walk to the nearby road junction. Keep straight ahead here; don't cross the dam. Continue for about 250m to find a gate on the right. Take this path, the Holme Valley Riverside Walk, as it descends steeply through woodland to join the reservoir service track. Follow this left to reach the main road at Holmbridge.

Turn right, pass the parish church and, on the next bend, take the road to the left,

signed for Yateholme. At the top of the hill, leave the road to turn left up Brownhill Lane, along the side of a house with a sundial on the gable end. In about 100m, where the road turns to the left at a group of houses, watch out for a gate by Kilnhouse Bank Farm. Go straight ahead here, past the side of the farm and up the hill beyond. The path steadily rises on the left-hand side of a lovely wooded clough. Towards the top, it crosses to the other side of the beck but keeps straight ahead before eventually curving round to a gate giving access to a walled lane. Turn right, now almost level along the hillside, close to a wall. After 400m a slight descent brings you to the corner of a plantation. Veer right here, going across a stile and descending a track alongside the small beck until it reaches the car park.

Tunnel End and March Haigh

Distance 8km **Time** 2 hours 30
Terrain towpath and moorland paths,
can be squelchy in places
Map OS Explorer OL21 **Access** buses (181,
184, 185) from Huddersfield and (181)
from Oldham to Marsden; trains from
Leeds and Manchester to Marsden

The transPennine canal and rail routes
converge as they travel through Marsden
but pass through separate tunnels at
Standedge. The 1812 Canal Tunnel was an
engineering feat of some significance on
its construction, but its life was short, as
the railway soon signalled the death
knell for inland waterways. Before the
advances in tunnelling techniques, the
old packhorse route of Rape's Highway
crossed the misty moors above. All are
visited on this traverse of the furthest
fringes of the Colne Valley.

Start from the National Trust car park
close to Marsden Railway Station. There is

a National Trust building here with lots of
interesting information on the area.
Follow the canal towpath towards the
tunnel for about 500m. Approaching
Tunnel End, take the access drive across
the canal, passing the visitor centre. It's
worth stopping in to see the exhibit on
the history of the canal and its restoration.

Just beyond the visitor centre, cross a
road. A footpath (signed for March Haigh)
goes to the right at the back of the house
opposite, just in front of an imposing
metal gate. From here, a lovely well-
surfaced path leads across the meadows.
Immediately after Orchard Hey Cottage,
turn right through a gate to follow the
footpath between houses, then veer left
onto a driveway beyond. Pass Berry Greave
and then, soon after the lane begins to
descend, turn right at a junction next to a
grit bin. Where this lane ends, continue
along the footpath beyond to cross the
hillside, dotted with hawthorn blossom

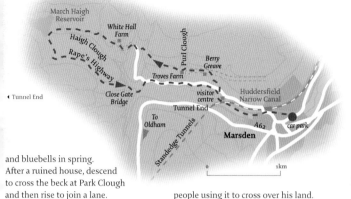

and bluebells in spring.
After a ruined house, descend
to cross the beck at Park Clough
and then rise to join a lane.

Turn right, signed for March Haigh.
Shortly after, bend left at a junction, then
keep going along the track past the drive
to White Hall Farm. A few metres past
this, leave the track, turning left over a
stile to follow the footpath across the
moor. The path weaves over the rough
ground, broadly parallel to Haigh Clough
down to the left. Cross a slab bridge over a
small beck and aim for the left-hand end
of March Haigh Reservoir dam wall, now
clear ahead.

The reservoir was built as a feeder
supply for the Huddersfield Narrow Canal
and has recently undergone extensive
restoration work. An information board
provides more details. From the board,
bear left along a path which soon joins a
disued leat and then comes to Rape's
Highway, an ancient packhorse route.
Running between Marsden and Rochdale,
the packhorse route was subject to a court
battle in the Edwardian era, when the
local Lord of the Manor sought to stop

people using it to cross over his land.
Happily, he lost and the route became a
public right of way. The Lord is surely
turning in his grave at the open access
now allowed on this land! Turn sharp left
to join the highway and follow the wide
track down to Eastergate Bridge at the
bottom of the moor. Officially known as
Close Gate Bridge, this graceful arched
bridge apparently got its colloquial name
from Esther Schofield, landlady of the pub
once on this site. It's a scheduled ancient
monument and is a beautiful spot to rest
for a while.

Cross the bridge and continue alongside
the beck to meet a road. Turn right for
about 400m and look for a gateway to a
waterside path, running parallel to the
road. As the path ends, don't go through
the gate back to the road. Instead, bear
right, going to the right of a row of
houses and descending a field. Cross a
lane and continue down to the Tunnel
End Visitor Centre. Return along the
towpath to the car park.

Wessenden Valley and Standedge

Distance 11km **Time** 3 hours
Terrain stony track for first section, then
moorland paths **Maps** OS Explorer OL1
and OL21 **Access** buses (181, 184, 185) from
Huddersfield to Marsden; trains from
Leeds and Manchester to Marsden

Depending on where you're standing, the
small town of Marsden is either the first
or last in Yorkshire. Historically, this has
always made it a key outpost for
travellers crossing the Pennine moors.
Historic turnpike tracks began their
ascent over the moors from this point,
while later developments funnelled the
railway and canal through here before
they plunged under the hills. The slopes
above the town are rich in historical
evidence of these routes, as well as the
more recent Pennine Way.

Start from the New Inn at the junction

of the A62 and Peel Street in the centre of
Marsden. Walk up Peel Street. At the top,
turn right into Carrs Road and at the
roundabout turn left into Binn Road,
signed for Wessenden. After about 600m,
take the signed public bridleway. Rise
steadily into the Wessenden Valley,
passing Butterley and Blakeley Reservoirs.
Soon after the latter, leave the track and
turn right onto the signed Pennine Way.

Descend steeply to cross Wessenden
Brook, then ascend Blakeley Clough,
lushly carpeted in bilberry. The gradient
eases later and the path crosses a
moorland plateau to reach Black Moss
Reservoir. Stay on the Pennine Way along
the dam wall, then bending left and soon
right. Crossing the brow of the hill, look
ahead to see Redbrook Reservoir and the
dome of Pule Hill.

Still above the reservoir, arrive at a

junction and turn sharp right, signed for Marsden, to leave the Pennine Way. A broad grassy route strides across the moorland area of Bobus. This is a former turnpike route, constructed by the remarkable 'Blind Jack' Metcalfe of Knaresborough. Follow the route until you reach Mount Road, turning left to walk along the road for about 500m. Before reaching the A62, bear right along a moorland footpath next to a sign for Marsden Moor and marker post for the Standedge Trail. Follow the path along the base of Pule Hill, with its serrated rocky edge up to the right. If you look carefully you may spot the Trog 'Ole, a natural arch in the gritstone. After about 600m, bear right up an old tramway incline, heading for the quarry at the top. A deviation into the quarry to your right is worthwhile; as well as the evocative ruins of ghostly industry, you will also find one of the Stanza Stones, featuring engraved poetry by Simon Armitage (the others are spread across West Yorkshire).

However, the route turns left at the head of the incline on a trod going slightly downhill. When this crosses a diagonal path, bear right and continue diagonally up the hill to reach the beginning of the summit plateau. Here, turn sharp right to follow a grassy path along the edge and over the top of Pule Hill, continuing steeply down the other side, back to the road.

Walk back along Mount Road for about 600m. Just before a cattle grid, bear left along Old Mount Road, then almost immediately bear left again to follow the track to Hades Farm. After 800m, the retaining wall veers down to the right and the footpath follows the side of this, leaving the track and passing a barn at a sign for a public footpath. Keep ahead, following the wall and then fence, to end up on a narrow path between houses. Turn left along the road to return to Marsden.

◀ Pule Hill

Scammonden

Distance 4.5km (or 6km with optional extension) Time 1 hour 30 (or 2 hours) Terrain well-maintained paths, tracks and lanes Map OS Explorer OL21 Access no public transport to the start

The reservoir at Scammonden is notable for having the first (and, so far, only) motorway dam in the UK. The surging transPennine traffic gets only a flickering view of the reservoir and valley beyond, but the walker has the chance to discover many more delights. Easy-going waterside paths allow you to explore the sailboat-spangled water and the valley's quieter corners.

Start at New Lane Car Park, the lower of two serving Scammonden reservoirs. Follow the path from the left-hand corner of the car park, past the sculpture of three sheep and into mixed woodland. Arriving at a path junction shortly afterwards, turn left over the footbridge crossing Blackburn Brook. Ascend the hillside here either by the steps or by using the sloped zigzag path. From here, the path rises above the reservoir and heads towards Dean Head Church, with views across to Scammonden Reservoir Sailing Club. The community once served by the church has now largely been submerged under the dark waters of the reservoir.

The young woodland around the church contains a diverse range of species, including apple, oak, rowan and silver birch, with bilberry, heather and broom carpeting the floor. There is historical interest, too: a sign on the left of the path marks the site of Styhill, a medieval settlement first mentioned in the Wakefield court rolls of 1324.

The distant swishing noise of traffic becomes louder as the M62 dam comes into view. The path rises up to meet a

◀ Scammonden

cycleway, right in front of the motorway, on the edge of the dam. Turn right, crossing the dam on the cycleway parallel to the motorway. This section is far from tranquil, but is only a short traverse and certainly has novelty value! While the presence of the motorway is an intrusion, it gives pause for thought on the many pressures on the South Pennines landscape, reminding us how valuable the quieter spaces are. Scammonden Reservoir reflects this pressure too, constructed to sate the growing thirst of Huddersfield in the late 1960s.

At the end of the dam, the path curves round to the right. Almost immediately afterwards, turn sharp right to wind downhill towards the water. The path levels out as you pass a tunnel under the motorway on your right; keep left along the side of the reservoir. Continue just above the water. Approaching the sailing club, the path turns to the left and climbs up to wind round above the premises, before descending to meet an access driveway. Turn left along this for about 200m and then turn right onto the signed Kirklees Way, down a tarmac track towards the water. Just before reaching the

slipway, turn left back onto the gravel waterside route to return to the car park.

If you want to continue this watery tour, take a short extension to the higher reservoir at Deanhead. To do so, continue from the car park, turning left up the lane. After 200m where the road bears left, turn right over a stile to join a cinder track. Head across the rough pasture towards the dam of Deanhead Reservoir. There is much more moorland scenery here, quite a contrast to the wooded bowl of Scammonden Reservoir. Turn right across a footbridge and cross the dam wall. At the far side of the dam, turn right to follow the Kirklees Way. When this path meets the lane, turn right and head downhill back to the car park.

Index